Bakerview Dairies

Managerial Applications of Cost Accounting
A Case Study of Bakerview Dairies

Paul Jeyakumar, *British Columbia Institute of Technology*
Shirley Mauger

PEARSON

Prentice
Hall

Toronto

Library and Archives Canada Cataloguing in Publication

Jeyakumar, Paul, 1948–
    Managerial applications of cost accounting : a case study of Bakerview
Dairies / Paul Jeyakumar, Shirley Mauger.

ISBN-13: 978-0-13-223564-8
ISBN-10: 0-13-223564-1

    1. Cost accounting. 2. Cost accounting--Case studies. I. Mauger, Shirley
II. Title.

HF5686.C8J49 2006
657'.42   C2006-903576-8

ISBN-10: 0-13-223564-1
ISBN-13: 978-0-13-223564-8

Editor-in-Chief, Business & Economics:
    Gary Bennett
Executive Acquisitions Editor: Samantha Scully
Executive Marketing Manager: Cas Shields
Senior Developmental Editor: Madhu Ranadive
Production Editor: Jen Handel
Copy Editor: Gail Marsden
Production Coordinator: Avinash Chandra
Composition: Deanne Walle
Photo/Permissions Research: Susan Wallace-Cox
Art Director: Julia Hall
Cover Design: David Cheung
Cover Image: Getty Images

Bakerview Dairies is a fictitious company. All facts and data referring to Bakerview have been created for the purposes of this instructional case study and do not represent any specific company's information. Any similarities to a real situation are only by coincidence. Graphs, data, and information relative to national statistics of dairy production, sales, and consumption in Canada are used by permission from various sources, including Statistics Canada, Agriculture and Agri-Food Canada, and Euromonitor.

Credits:
Page 10: Figure 2: data adapted from Statistics Canada CANSIM database, Table 002-0011; page 10: Figure 3: data adapted from Euromonitor International; page 11: Figure 4: data adapted from Statistics Canada CANSIM database, Table 002-0011; page 12: Figure 5: data adapted from Statistics Canada CANSIM database, Table 002-0011; pages 9–13 (as cited in footnotes): *Sector Profile: Ice Cream*, http://www.dairyinfo.gc.ca/ pdf_files/prof_milk_e.pdf, Agriculture and Agri-Food Canada – Dairy Section, 2004. Reproduced with the permission of the Minister of Public Works and Government Services, [2006], and *Sector Profile: Milk and Cream*, http://www.dairyinfo.gc.ca/ pdf_files/prof_milk_e.pdf, Agriculture and Agri-Food Canada – Dairy Section, 2004. Reproduced with the permission of the Minister of Public Works and Government Services, [2006].

Statistics Canada information is used with the permission of Statistics Canada. Users are forbidden to copy this material and/or redisseminate the data, in an original or modified form, for commercial purposes, without the expressed permission of Statistics Canada. Information on the availability of the wide range of data from Statistics Canada can be obtained form Statistics Canada's Regional Offices, its World Wide Web site at http://www.statscan.ca, and its toll-free access number 1-800-263-1136.

3 4 5   15 14 13 12

Printed and bound in Canada.

CONTENTS

Bakerview Dairies

NORMA RIVAS

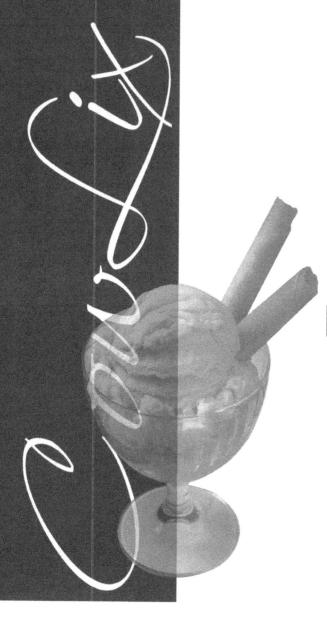

INTRODUCTION

MANAGERIAL ACCOUNTING AND ICE CREAM?

What do managerial accounting and ice cream have in common? Learning the tools and concepts of managerial accounting is a good first step in understanding the complex task of planning, leading and managing an organization. Applying these tools to assist in making better decisions adds value for the learner when practical applications are made available.

This is where the ice cream comes in. This case study will introduce you to the strategies and managerial accounting practices of a Canadian midsize food processing operation. The company is Bakerview Dairies. You will focus on its ice cream manufacturing division by responding to the issues and requests outlined in the case study. While the company is fictitious, care has been taken to provide you with facts and figures that are typical of this industry.

The case study provides you with an opportunity to combine your knowledge of managerial accounting tools with problem solving and Excel spreadsheet skills for an assessment of Bakerview Dairies' cost accounting system and its strategic direction.

What will you learn?

Depending on the number of modules your instructor requires you to complete, you will gain experience in the following areas:

- **Practical application of selected managerial accounting tools**. The following topics are covered using 'real life' applications:

  - Strategy
  - Cost of goods manufactured; Cost of goods sold
  - Cost volume profit analysis
  - Overhead application
  - Activity based costing and preparation of the income statement using the activity based approach
  - Choice of cost drivers; Regression analysis
  - Budget preparation and variance analysis
  - Absorption and variable costing
  - Theory of constraints: Linear Programming (Solver)
  - Special orders and outsourcing decisions
  - Inventory Management
  - Customer profitability analysis
  - Cost allocations – Support costs
  - Cost allocations – Joint costs
  - Pricing
  - Capital budgeting
  - Benchmarking
  - Performance evaluations
  - Strategy evaluation using ROI, RI and ROS
  - The balanced scorecard

- **Use of Excel as a management decision support tool to assess cost accounting systems**. The modules provide you with opportunities to develop decision support models using Excel. Combined with extended/advanced Excel applications such as regression analysis and linear programming you will apply practical management science techniques to a business environment.

- **Application of problem solving skills.** You will use general business knowledge as well as general problem solving skills in order to analyze many facets of the organization and determine the best plan of action.

- **Ability to communicate both orally and in writing.** You will have the opportunity to document and periodically present your findings and conclusions as you would in a business environment.

CASE CONTENTS

Modules

The Bakerview Dairies case study is presented in the following eleven modules:

1. **Bakerview Dairies and the Ice Cream Industry**
   - An introduction to the project that presents background information on the company, its products and the industry. The module requires research and identification of the external factors that influence the company's operation.

2. **Preliminary Analysis**
   - The preparation of the statement of cost of goods manufactured, and the income statement.
   - The use of the contribution margin approach, and managerial decision making using cost volume profit analysis.

3. **Focus on Activities**
   - The application of activity based costing and activity based management principles to the company's manufacturing processes. Use of regression analysis for the selection of appropriate cost drivers.

4. **Assessing Feedback**
   - The use of master budgets, the creation of flexible budget and variance analyses.

5. **Inventory and Income**
   - The impact of inventory costing methods on income determination when absorption costing and variable costing approaches are used.

6. **Allocating Resources**
   - The use of relevant information in decision making and managing limited resources with a view to maximizing profit. Use of Excel Solver to determine an optimal production plan.

7. **Allocating Costs**
   - The allocation of support department costs to operating departments and joint product costs to individual products.

8. **Analyzing Costs and Profitability**
   - The management of inventory and analysis of customer profitability.

9. **Pricing for Profits**
   - The approaches used in setting prices using market-based and cost-based methods.

10. **Investing for Profits**
    - Planning for capital budgeting with emphasis on the net present value method.

11. **Evaluating Success**
    - Benchmarking and assessment of the company's strategies through performance evaluation using ROI, RI, ROS.
    - Using the balanced scorecard to measure and evaluate the company's strategies.
    - A comprehensive recommendation on issues that have been identified in modules 1 through 10.

CASE PROCESS

Modules

Each module consists of the following sections:

Emphasis and
Outcomes

- A section entitled 'Emphasis and Outcomes' listing the key topics and the learning outcomes upon completion of the module.

Case Events

- Sections that present case events simulating the events that can take place in any organization. The situations described under various headings in the main body of each module provide the facts and issues faced by the personnel of Bakerview Dairies' ice cream processing division. You are required to analyze these situations and provide recommendations.

You Are In Control

- A section entitled 'You Are in Control' which lists the activities that are to be completed for that portion of the case. Your instructor will identify which activities you will complete and may provide you with an alternative activity.

Bakerview Dairies

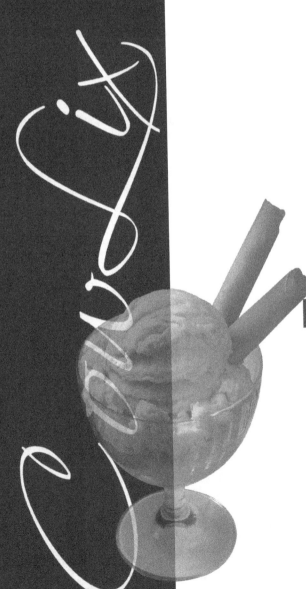

Module 1
Bakerview and the Ice Cream Industry

EMPHASIS AND OUTCOMES

The emphasis of this module is on obtaining background information on the company, its products and the industry.

At the end of this module you should be able to:
- Relate the marketing issues in the ice cream and fluid milk industry to Bakerview Dairies.
- Explain how current events can affect a company's goals and strategies.
- List the major steps in ice cream production.
- Identify at least five major ingredients of ice cream.
- Define the industry terminology.

OVERVIEW

Every year millions of Canadians enjoy the flavour of ice cream. TJ Conner, the owner and president of Bakerview Dairies, is counting on having more Canadians enjoy the flavour of 'Cowlix Natural Ice Cream,' Bakerview's featured brand name product. Cowlix was introduced in 1995 and continues to enjoy steady growth in local markets. Many consumers like both the taste of Cowlix and the fact that the Cowlix brand's ingredients come from dairy cows that are given natural vitamin supplements instead of those with synthetic additives. Bakerview also ensures that their ice cream contains a lower percentage of fat than the competitor's product. This, along with their wacky and exotic flavours, 'Moose Madness' and 'Chai High,' have given the company a competitive advantage in the premium ice cream niche market.

To date, success has been noteworthy. The company has managed a steady growth in sales since it began its operations. It has also maintained a sound financial basis of profitable growth, increasing value for the shareholders and creating career opportunities and financial rewards for its employees. The management has also been actively involved in local community events and social needs programs.

"…their wacky and exotic flavours, 'Moose Madness' and 'Chai High,' have given the company a competitive advantage in the premium ice cream niche market."

Yet TJ, the owner, is not complacent about the success of the company. He has recently been very proactive in the management of the company and has continually been monitoring progress and scrutinizing costs taking care to analyze variances. He is concerned that the ice cream industry may face a diminishing market. He feels that issues such as obesity and trans-fats may reduce industry-wide consumer demand for ice cream.

When the company launched its operation in 1995, its intention was to break into the market by selling the finest quality low fat, all-natural ice cream in a wide variety of innovative flavours made from local dairy products. This, according to TJ, would provide the company with a sustainable competitive advantage.

TJ has just finished a meeting with the company controller, Pat Duco, in which the quarterly reports were discussed. The results for Cowlix are not as optimistic as TJ had hoped for. While sales have increased, the reported profit margins for some products have not shown significant increase during this quarter. In the meeting, Pat emphasized to TJ that the main reason for falling profit margins was the rising costs of ingredients. Yet, TJ is not convinced that they are 'at the mercy' of rising costs of raw materials. He is convinced that a further analysis of the situation is necessary.

COMPANY BACKGROUND

Bakerview Dairies was established by four local dairy producers in 1980 as the Mt. Baker Milk Company. TJ Conner and Al Haagen were part of the original consortium of four. Initially their mission was to process and market fluid homogenized milk to local grocery stores, markets and restaurants. TJ had the business skills to develop the financial and administrative aspects of the business, and Al had the entrepreneurial and marketing background to distribute the product. While the other two dairy producers were directors, they were content to let TJ and Al run the day to day operations.

In 1990, the other two producers sold their share of the business to TJ and Al, who at that time decided to turn their existing farming operations over to their sons in order to expand the processing plant.

"TJ and Al discovered that ice cream production was an economical complement to fluid milk processing."

In 1995, after extensive research, Mt. Baker Milk Company changed its name to Bakerview Dairies. TJ and Al discovered that ice cream production was an economical complement to fluid milk processing. Therefore they decided to add ice cream under the brand name, Cowlix, to their product mix. Their existing plant already had some of the processing equipment such as pasteurizers and homogenizers. Initially, relatively little equipment had to be added to the plant: mixers, ice cream freezers and filling equipment and coolers for hardening and storing the ice cream. The cream that was removed from the raw milk before bottling in the fluid milk processing division became the main ingredient for the ice cream.

The demand for their new brand of ice cream made it necessary for TJ and Al to implement a separate and automated production line for ice cream in 1997. With the help of Jared Benot, who was an experienced operations manager, they were able to install the highly technical equipment. This allowed them to increase production without having to hire additional staff in the manufacturing area.

Today, Bakerview Dairies operates two separate divisions: the milk processing division and the ice cream division. Both divisions share the same owner; however most of its resources and information systems are separate. While the focus of this study is on the ice cream division, pertinent facts relating to the milk processing division will be provided as needed.

Currently, Bakerview Dairies' ice cream division, which solely produces the Cowlix brand, is operating at 80% capacity. The ice cream production line churns out about 1.5 million litres of ice cream per year, while fluid milk production fills approximately 8 million litres of milk annually. The company has a production staff of 30 and an administrative staff of 10. Some of the staff work full time for the ice cream division. Other staff members work in both the milk processing division and the ice cream division. Figure 1 illustrates the functional responsibilities of the ice cream division.

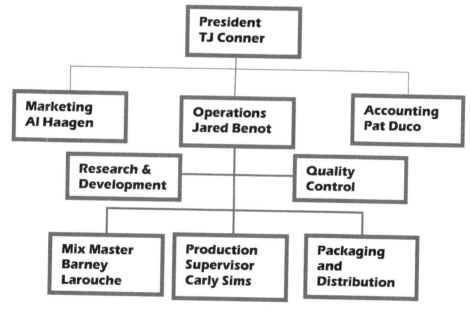

Figure 1: Organization Chart – BAKERVIEW DAIRIES
Ice Cream Division

THE INDUSTRY

Ice Cream

Ice cream[1] is the product obtained from freezing a mixture of pasteurized milk, cream and sugar. It can be flavoured with fruit, fruit juice or an extract (chocolate, vanilla, etc.). It is the only frozen food that can be cut, scooped or sliced, and consumed at a temperature below 0°C. Ice cream is made up of an average of 50% air and 27-32% water. Minimum contents for milk fat and milk solids are defined in the Canadian Food and Drugs Act. The Act also sets out standards for ice milk and sorbets, which are characterized, among other things, by a lower milk fat content than ice cream.

Canadian production of hard ice cream has remained below 300 million litres since 2000. In 2004, Canadian processors made 284.5 million litres of hard ice cream.

About 1,557 workers in 61 Canadian plants make ice cream and frozen desserts. These products generated sales worth $644.7 million in 2002. The Canadian ice cream industry is dominated by Nestlé and Unilever. In fact, these two companies hold a 27.9% and 22.8% share of the market respectively. Smaller companies, such as Chapman, also hold a share of the market. Processors innovate by offering more and more "good for your health" products as well as high-end ice creams, rich in cream and made from natural ingredients.

Consumption Trends – Ice Cream

As illustrated in Figure 2[2], ice cream consumption is decreasing in Canada. It has remained below 12 litres per capita per year since 1987. Consumption reached its lowest level in 2000, at 8.74 litres per capita. Since then, it increased slightly then slumped again, reaching 9.28 litres per capita in 2004. Sherbet and ice milk (ice cream substitutes), lag far behind, with annual consumption in 2004 of 0.29 litres and 1.96 litres per capita, respectively. However, consumption of ice milk has increased by 33.3% in the past 10 years. Annual consumption of frozen products is related to summer weather conditions. Hot summers with heat waves are more conducive to the consumption of frozen products than cooler summers.

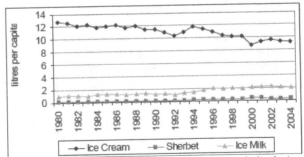

Figure 2: Consumption of ice cream, ice milk and sherbet

---

[1] Information in the following sections are reproduced from *Sector Profile: Ice Cream*, http://www.dairyinfo.gc.ca/pdf_files/prof_icecream_e.pdf, Agriculture and Agri-Food Canada—Dairy Section, 2004 (accessed January 2005).
[2] *Sector Profile: Ice Cream*, p. 2; data in figure adapted from Statistics Canada.

Retail Sales

Figure 3[3] shows the volumes of ice cream and frozen yogurt sold in the same period. Ice cream sold in family size containers is very popular, although individual serving sizes are gaining in popularity, with a 6.9% increase since 2001. Although frozen yogurt accounts for only 3.7% of sales, this product has seen the most growth, with volumes sold increasing by 8.3% between 2001 and 2004.[4]

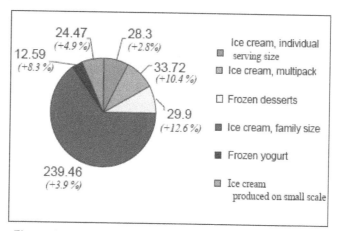

Figure 3: Volume (in million tonnes) and percentage variation (compared with 2001) in ice cream and frozen yogurt sales in Canada, 2004

Milk

In the Canadian dairy industry,[5] raw milk can be processed either as fluid milk or as industrial milk. Fluid milk is processed to produce liquids such as pasteurized milk, skim milk, sterilized milk and table cream. Industrial milk is used to manufacture products that are not liquid, such as yogurt, cheese, evaporated milk, butter, ice cream, etc.

Canadian milk production, illustrated in Figure 4[6], has been quite stable for the past four years, holding steady at above 2,600 million litres. The amount of milk produced in each category varied little between 2001 and 2004.

[3] *Sector Profile: IceCream*, p. 2; data in figure adapted from Euromonitor.

[4] *Sector Profile: Ice Cream*, p. 2; data in figure adapted from Statistics Canada.

[5] Information in the following sections are reproduced from *Sector Profile: Milk and Cream*, http://www.dairyinfo.gc.ca/pdf_files/ prof_milk_e.pdf, Agriculture and Agri-Food Canada—Dairy Section, 2004 (accessed January 2005), p. 1.

[6] *Sector Profile: Milk*, p. 2; data in figure adapted from Statistics Canada.

Fluid milk is processed throughout Canada in 178 plants that employ some 5,973 workers. Cash receipts generated from the sale of milk and cream from farms to processors totaled $4,591 million in 2004. The industry is dominated by three main players, Agropur, Parmalat Canada and Saputo. Agropur is a dairy cooperative, owned by 4,203 dairy farmers. Natrel, the milk and cream division of Agropur, processes 44.1% of all the milk processed by the cooperative (781 million litres). This division employs 1,540 workers at three plants in Ontario, four in Quebec and one in British Columbia. Agropur holds about 25.6% of the Canadian fluid milk market. In 2004, Agropur acquired Island Farm Dairy Co-operative of British Columbia and its two plants (including one that processes fluid milk.)

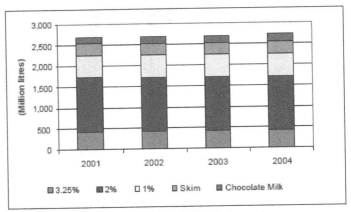

Figure 4: Milk Production in Canada

Parmalat Canada, a subsidiary of the Parmalat Group based in Italy, holds about 15.5% of the fluid milk market in Canada. Parmalat has three milk processing plants in Ontario, two in Quebec, one in Alberta and one in Manitoba.

The Saputo milk division's sales rose in 2004. A large part of this division's income comes from the retail sector (80%), while foodservices account for 20% of its income. Saputo relies on niche products for its growth. The company markets the Dairyland brands in Ontario and the West, Nutrilait in Quebec and Baxter in the Maritime Provinces.

Neilson Dairy, owned by George Weston Ltd, processes fluid milk and several other products (yogurt, sour cream). The company has two plants in Ontario.

Both the Maritime Provinces and British Columbia are served mainly by co-operatives such as Central Dairies in Newfoundland, Farmers Dairy in Nova Scotia, Amalgamated Dairies Limited in Prince Edward Island, and Northumberland Cooperative Dairy Limited in New Brunswick.

Consumption Trends - Milk

The total annual consumption of milk in Canada, as illustrated in Figure 5[7], is on the decline since the 1980s. As of 2004, it was 85.2 litres per capita.

Consumption of homogenized milk (3.25%) and 2% milk has dropped by 40.3% and 29.5% respectively since 1990, while 1% partly skimmed milk, skim and chocolate milk are increasingly popular with Canadians. Consumption of 1% milk has increased by 206% since 1990, reaching 17.9 litres per capita in 2004. The consumption of skim milk rose slightly in 2004, to 8.63 litres per capita. Chocolate milk is the least consumed type of milk in the country. However, its consumption is increasing and reached an average of 5.4 litres per capita in 2004.

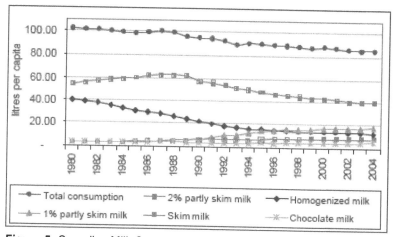

Figure 5: Canadian Milk Consumption

Statistics Canada does not compile data on consumption of milk products enriched with calcium or omega-3 fatty acids. However, these increasingly popular products are meeting consumer demands for foods with special health benefits.

Consumers are also offered a wide range of packaging (plastic bottles, cartons with caps, individual servings, etc.).

Retail Sales

Retail sales of milk are on the decline in Canada. In fact, there was a drop of 4.5% in the quantities of milk sold between 2001 and 2004. Only sales of goat's milk and fat-free milk increased during this period.

The average price in today's dollars of a litre of homogenized milk increased by 10.3% between 2001 and 2004, while the price of a litre of partially skimmed milk increased by 10%.

---

[7] *Sector Profile: Milk and Cream*, p. 2; data in figure adapted from Statistics Canada.

THE PRODUCTS

Milk

Bakerview Dairies' fluid milk processing division is well known for its farm fresh milk. The motto of the company is 'Naturally' and its labels reflect a retro 1960s look in order to emphasize its organic product. In order to simplify the production process, the company only produces homogenized milk in four-litre plastic containers. The product is distributed to local restaurants, independently owned grocers, fruit and vegetable markets and a number of Canadian grocery chains. While the price is usually two to five cents higher than the competition, shoppers are willing to purchase Bakerview Dairies' milk because of its perceived quality.

Ice Cream

Cowlix ice cream is the flagship product of Bakerview Dairies' ice cream division. Before venturing into this product line in 1995, TJ and Al thoroughly researched the industry. They realized that the key to success was to hire an individual who knew the science of ice cream mixing. They interviewed a number of ice cream experts to find one who excelled in the field. They hired Barney Larouche, who had spent a number of years working at a major ice cream producer in the eastern United States, creating award winning flavours.

With Barney's experience they were able to create organic low fat ice cream in a variety of flavours that tasted like the premium varieties with high fat content that were currently being marketed. To date, no one has been able to copy their recipe, and as a result their brand name has gained more popularity across Canada. Most Canadian grocery chains carry the Cowlix brand. The product is marketed in litre containers and is normally shelved in the same area as premium ice creams.

PROCESSES AND THE MASTER BUDGET

Manufacturing Processes

TASK

Pat Duco, the controller, has hired you to provide your managerial accounting advice in various areas of Bakerview Dairies' ice cream division. In your first meeting with Pat, she provides you with more details of the processes that are in place to control the flow of information and record costs for manufacturing ice cream. The first document she hands you is a copy of the manufacturing process chart. (See Table 1 at the end of this module.) This chart illustrates the steps involved in producing ice cream from the receipt of raw materials to freezing the ice cream in the hardening tunnel at the end of the production run.

> *"The production process involves several operations in which conversion costs and ingredients are added to the product."*

Ice cream production involves like or similar units or batches. As such, a process costing system is used[8]. The batches, which consist of 4000 litres of ice cream, are processed in a similar manner and receive the same amount of direct labour costs, basic ingredients, and manufacturing overhead costs. Therefore these costs are averaged over all batches.

The production process involves several operations in which conversion costs and ingredients are added to the product. Ingredients are added at the beginning of each operation requiring the basic mix, sauces, and particulates. Direct labour costs and overhead are added evenly throughout the process.

Master Budget

Process Costing
process identical
products, so 2 things
DM or something else

Ordering costing
Process things with
customer's specifications

Pat also presents you with the next set of documents, which is the operations portion of the master budget for the year just completed. (See the Appendix.) The sales forecast was based on the previous year's demand plus an additional percentage to account for the forecast increase in demand. The budget was developed by:

- Al Haagen, Marketing Manager
- Jared Benot, Operations Manager
- Pat Duco, Controller
- TJ Conner, President

These personnel are accountable for the plans and strategies for the company. They develop the master budget based on input from their employees.

When assessing the budget you should note the following:

- Bakerview Dairies' fiscal year end is December 31.

- Bakerview uses a standard costing system to evaluate performance. The first table in the master budget is the 'Standards for Mix and Cost of Materials' schedule which sets the standards by which actual performance is measured.

- Sales demand is highest in summer with another peak in demand during the Christmas holiday season.

- Beginning and ending finished goods and ingredients (raw materials) inventory remain fairly constant throughout the year. As a result, inventory levels are not considered in the budget.

- There is no work in process inventory. The batch process is complete when ice cream is packaged and hardened. This process is normally complete at the end of each day.

---

[8]To reduce complexity in the case study, process costing is used. A batch system, such as ice cream production, would normally use an operational costing system which is a hybrid of process and job costing.

- The budget is based on 80% of operational capacity.

- Manufacturing overhead is applied to the product based on direct labour dollar.

- The cost driver for commissions, delivery, and shipping is litres.

FACILITIES

BAKERVIEW DAIRIES – FLUID MILK AND ICE CREAM PROCESSING DIVISIONS	
Plant Size:	20,000 square feet
Employees:	27 production employees, two maintenance mechanics, one maintenance engineer
Volume:	Ice cream: 1.5 million litres a year Fluid milk: 4.5 million litres a year
Product Lineup:	Ice cream (3 flavours) and fluid milk
Packages:	Round litres – ice cream 4-litre plastic jugs – fluid milk
Fillers:	one round litre filler 4-litre jug filler
Ice Cream Mix Lines:	One
Freezer Lines:	One blast freezer
Bottling Lines:	One
Pasteurizing Vats:	Three 2000-litre vats
Raw Storage:	Cream and condensed skim (two 10,000-litre tanks, one 16,000-litre tank)
Sucrose:	One 10,000-litre tank
Pasteurized Storage:	Three 9,000-litre tanks, one 3,000-litre tank
Hardening Tunnel:	Tri tray (5,000 litres per hour)

(handwritten annotations: "Indirect labour costs", "Output", "output", "DM", "machine")

YOU ARE IN CONTROL

Before you assess Bakerview Dairies' current cost accounting system you need to research the industry facts, trends and current events in addition to finding valuable resources that can be used in analyzing this company. The following is a list of activities that will assist in your research.

**Activity 1
Ice Cream
Production**

Learn about the process of ice cream production, and prepare a flowchart illustrating the process. Compare your results with the chart given at the end of this module.

Ben and Jerry's Ice Cream in Vermont, USA has a good overview of ice cream production. You can view this presentation at:
http://www.benjerry.com/fun_stuff/cow_to_cone/

**Activity 2
Fluid Milk
Production**

Learn about the pasteurization and homogenization process for fluid milk and prepare a flowchart illustrating this process.

HINT: The University of Guelph website has information on this process.

**Activity 3
Ice Cream
Ingredients**

Quality Ingredients
Quality ingredients are the key to creating quality ice cream. Identify the main ingredients of ice cream.

Questions you should be able to answer:
- Which ingredients require larger quantities?
- What is the shelf life of ingredients?
- Which ingredients will be more difficult to source?
- Which ingredients will require more working capital?
- What does the term 'overrun' mean in the ice cream industry?

In your discussion include at least two websites that you used to find this information.

**Activity 4
Industry
Events**

Current Events in the Industry
Identify current events in the news (within the last three years) that have or will have an effect on the ice cream and fluid milk industry. You should include at least one Canadian event and one global event. You may want to research such things as consumption, cost of ingredients, sources of ingredients, etc.

Questions you should be able to answer:
- What effect does this have on the industry in general?
- What effect will this have on Bakerview Dairies?

In your discussion include:
- The URL and name of the websites where you found this information
- Date of the article

Activity 5
Strategy and
Benchmarking

Company Strategy

Identify Bakerview Dairies' strategy. Research at least two other dairies of comparable size on the Internet. Include their name and URL in your discussion. Are their strategies similar?

Questions you should be able to answer:
- What are Bakerview's capabilities?
- Who are its competitors and where are they located?
- Are there substitute products on the market?
- Has Bakerview differentiated its products? If so, how?
- Do you agree with this strategy? If so, why do you agree? If not, what do you think the company should change?
- How is its strategy similar to or different from the other dairies you have researched?

A P P E N D I X : I C E   C R E A M   P R O C E S S I N G

Table 1: Ice Cream Processing

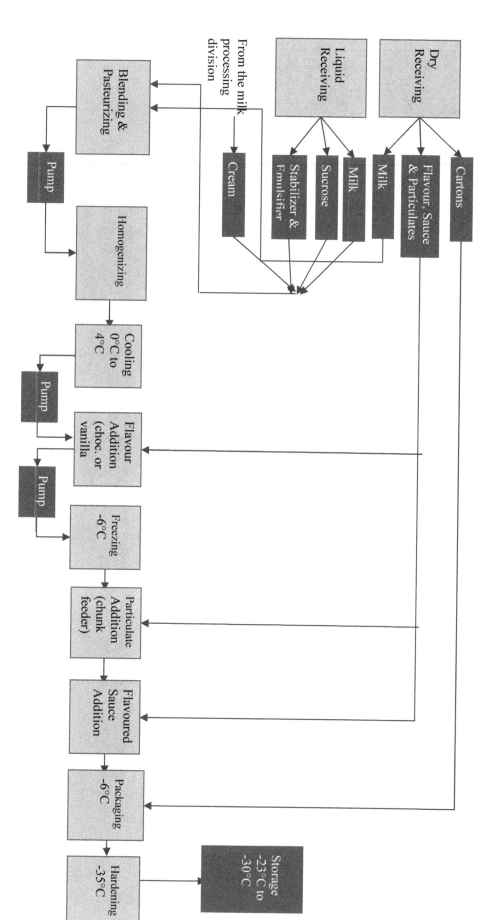

A P P E N D I X : M A S T E R B U D G E T

20

Bakerview Dairies – Partial Master Budget
Ice Cream Division

STANDARDS FOR MIX AND COST OF MATERIALS (per 1000 litres)

Frozen measure*	1000 litres Price	Per	VANILLA % in mix	Cost per 1000	MOOSE MADNESS % in mix	Cost per 1000	CHAI HIGH % in mix	Cost per 1000
Ingredients								
Cream	$4.00	litre	16.00%	$640.00	12.50%	$500.00	13.50%	$540.00
Sucrose	$0.65	litre	7.05%	$45.83	5.75%	$37.38	6.25%	$40.63
Stabilizer & emulsifier	$3.50	litre	0.30%	$10.50	0.25%	$8.75	0.25%	$8.75
Fluid milk	$58.20	hectolitre+	23.00%	$133.86	18.00%	$104.76	20.00%	$116.40
Milk powder	$5.30	kilogram	2.50%	$132.50	2.00%	$106.00	2.00%	$106.00
Vanilla	$70.00	litre	1.15%	$805.00	0.50%	$350.00	0.50%	$350.00
Variegate sauce	$6.00	litre	0.00%	$0.00	7.50%	$450.00	7.50%	$450.00
Particulate	$7.00	litre	0.00%	$0.00	3.50%	$245.00	0.00%	$0.00
Overrun (Air)	$0.00		50.00%	$0.00	50.00%	$0.00	50.00%	$0.00
Cost per 1000 litres			**100.0%**	**$1,767.69**	**100.0%**	**$1,801.89**	**100.0%**	**$1,611.78**

*1000 litres of ice cream starts with 500 litres of liquid measure. Overrun (the addition of air in the production process) of 100% results in 1000 litres of finished product.
+a hectolitre is equal to 100 litres

Schedule 1 - SALES & PRODUCTION BUDGET (Litres)*
For year ended December 31

	Quarter 1	Quarter 2	Quarter 3	Quarter 4	TOTAL
		*Litres to Produce/Sell			
Vanilla	160,000	164,000	180,000	160,000	664,000
Moose Madness	110,000	112,000	124,000	110,000	456,000
Chai High	63,000	64,000	70,000	63,000	260,000
TOTAL LITRES					1,380,000

*Beginning and ending inventories of ingredients and finished goods remain at the same levels, therefore sales equals production.

Schedule 2 - SALES and PRODUCTION BUDGET (Dollars)
For year ended December 31

(see schedule 1 for litres sold/produced)	Sell. Price /litre	Revenue				
		Quarter 1	Quarter 2	Quarter 3	Quarter 4	TOTAL
Vanilla	$3.96	$ 633,600	$ 649,440	$ 712,800	$ 633,600	$2,629,440
Moose Madness	$4.25	467,500	476,000	527,000	467,500	1,938,000
Chai High	$4.75	299,250	304,000	332,500	299,250	1,235,000
TOTAL SALES		$1,400,350	$1,429,440	$1,572,300	$1,400,350	$5,802,440

Schedule 3 - COST OF INGREDIENTS USED BUDGET
For the year ended December 31

	price per	Vanilla		Moose Madness		Chai High		TOTAL	
		Quantity	Cost	Quantity	Cost	Quantity	Cost	Quantity	Cost
Annual litre sales (schedule 1)		664,000		456,000		260,000		1,380,000	
Cream	$4.00 litre	106,240	$ 424,960	57,000	$ 228,000	35,100	$140,400	198,340	$ 793,360
Sucrose	$0.65 litre	46,812	30,428	26,220	17,043	16,250	10,563	89,282	58,033
Stabilizer & emulsifier	$3.50 litre	1,992	6,972	1,140	3,990	650	2,275	3,782	13,237
Fluid milk	$58.20 hectolitre+	1,527	88,883	821	47,771	520	30,264	2,868	166,918
Milk powder	$5.30 kilogram	16,600	87,980	9,120	48,336	5,200	27,560	30,920	163,876
Vanilla	$70.00 litre	7,636	534,520	2,280	159,600	1,300	91,000	11,216	785,120
Variegate sauce	$6.00 litre	-	-	34,200	205,200	19,500	117,000	53,700	322,200
Particulate	$7.00 litre	-	-	15,960	111,720	-	-	15,960	111,720
TOTAL COST OF INGREDIENTS			$ 1,173,743		$ 821,660		$419,062		$2,414,464

+a hectolitre is equal to 100 litres

Schedule 4 - DIRECT MANUFACTURING LABOUR BUDGET
For the year ended December 31

	Vanilla	Moose Madness	Chai High	TOTAL
Number of litres (schedule 3)	664,000	456,000	260,000	1,380,000
Batch size (litres)	4,000	4,000	4,000	4,000
Number of batches	166	114	65	345
Labour hours per batch	27.50	27.50	27.50	27.50
Total labour hours	4,565	3,135	1,788	9,488
Cost per labour hour	$ 32.41	$ 32.41	$ 32.41	$ 32.41
TOTAL DIRECT LABOUR COST	$147,952	$ 101,605	$ 57,933	$ 307,490

Schedule 5 - PACKAGING COSTS BUDGET
For year ended December 31

	Vanilla	Moose Madness	Chai High	TOTAL
Number of litres (schedule 1)	664,000	456,000	260,000	1,380,000
Packaging cost per litre	$ 0.17	$ 0.17	$ 0.17	$ 0.17
TOTAL PACKAGING COST	$ 112,880	$ 77,520	$ 44,200	$ 234,600

Schedule 6 - MANUFACTURING OVERHEAD BUDGET
For the year ended December 31

Variable		
Plant utilities	$ 146,000	
Equipment maintenance	130,000	$ 276,000
Fixed		
Quality control	150,000	
Computer and supplies	274,000	
Plant equipment amortization	246,000	
Research & development	180,000	
Salary and wages (Indirect)	218,146	
Plant lease	312,000	1,380,146
TOTAL MANUFACTURING OVERHEAD		$1,656,146
Total manufacturing overhead	$ 1,656,146	
Applied at budgeted level of direct labour dollars (schedule 4)	$ 307,490	is equal to $ 5.39 Overhead application rate per direct labour dollar

Manufacturing overhead applied	Vanilla	Moose Madness	Chai High	Total
Direct labour dollars (schedule 4)	$ 147,952	$ 101,605	$ 57,933	307,490
Application rate per direct labour dollar	$ 5.39	$ 5.39	$ 5.39	5.39
OVERHEAD APPLIED	$ 796,870	$ 547,248	$ 312,028	1,656,146

23

Schedule 7 - BUDGETED COST OF GOODS SOLD
For the year ended December 31

	Vanilla	Moose Madness	Chai High	Total
Ingredients used (Schedule 3)	$1,173,743	$821,660	$ 419,062	$ 2,414,465
Packaging costs (Schedule 5)	$ 112,880	$ 77,520	$ 44,200	$ 234,600
Direct labour (Schedule 4)	$ 147,952	$101,605	$ 57,933	$ 307,490
Manufacturing overhead (Schedule 6)	$ 796,870	$547,248	$ 312,028	$ 1,656,146
Cost of Goods Sold	**$2,231,445**	**$1,548,033**	**$ 833,222**	**$ 4,612,700**

Schedule 8 - OTHER COSTS BUDGET
For the year ended December 31

Variable Costs:		
Commissions	$140,000	
Delivery and shipping	47,000	
TOTAL OTHER VARIABLE COSTS		$ 187,000
Fixed Costs:		
Salaries	$436,000	
Interest and bank charges	45,000	
Professional fees	29,000	
Advertising and promotion	59,000	
Admin. computer services	31,390	
Miscellaneous expense	11,610	
Total Other Fixed Costs		$ 612,000
TOTAL OTHER COSTS		$ 799,000

25

Schedule 9 - BUDGETED INCOME STATEMENT
For the year ended December 31

	Vanilla	Moose Madness	Chai High	Total
Sales (Schedule 2)	$ 2,629,440	$1,938,000	$1,235,000	$ 5,802,440
Cost of goods sold (Schedule 7)	$ 2,231,445	$1,548,033	$ 833,222	$ 4,612,700
Gross margin	$ 397,995	$ 389,967	$ 401,778	$ 1,189,740
Other costs (Schedule 8)				$ 799,000
BUDGETED OPERATING INCOME				$ 390,740
Gross margin %	15.1%	20.1%	32.5%	20.5%

Bakerview Dairies

Module 2
Preliminary Analysis

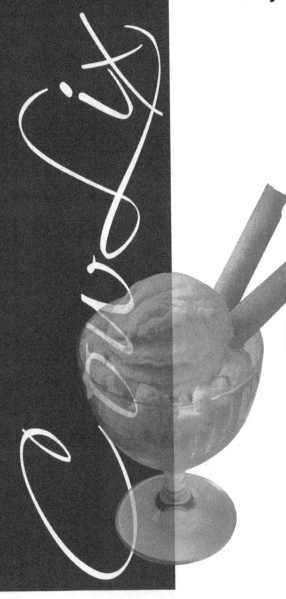

EMPHASIS AND OUTCOMES

The emphasis of this module is on the statement of cost of goods manufactured, the income statement, cost volume profit analysis and the use of the contribution margin in managerial decisions.

At the end of this module you should be able to:
- Develop a cost of goods manufactured statement and income statement.
- Classify costs incurred as period and product costs.
- Use cost volume profit analysis to assess alternatives and make decisions that will improve a company's profitability.
- Differentiate between gross margin and contribution margin and recognize how each is used to assess a company's profitability.
- Explain the importance of taking into consideration both the financial and non-financial effects of decision making.

GATHERING THE FACTS ...

Pat Duco, controller for Bakerview Dairies, is looking nervously at the clock in her office. It is early Tuesday afternoon and she knows that TJ Conner (President) is expecting the third quarter reports for the ice cream division on his desk by Wednesday. TJ wants to preview the results before the Monday morning meeting. Based on the previous quarter's results, TJ is closely following Bakerview's profit margins and Pat knows that he will be concerned with this quarter's figures. TJ prefers to review the income statement on paper before the meeting. However, the computer will not produce the financial reports.

Although the financial reports cannot be produced, Pat is aware that according to the preliminary reports, some product lines are not showing reasonable gross profit margins. She has to be prepared to explain the results and make recommendations for improving the profit margins of the company.

Ice Cream Division Background

In 1994, Al Haagen (Marketing) saw opportunities in diversifying Bakerview Dairies' operations by expanding into ice cream production. Ice cream is a natural fit for Bakerview because cream is a byproduct of their milk processing line. After researching the opportunity, Al and TJ learned that the ice cream industry offered stable profit margins and demand, with little direct local competition.

Today ice cream production operates in a separate division from fluid milk production. The Cowlix brand of ice cream was patented in November 1995 and began production in January 1996. Manufacturing started with Vanilla, and in 1999, an expert ice cream mix master was hired who developed their famous Moose Madness and Chai High varieties.

Cost of goods manufactured
Income Statement.

Moose Madness is a chocolate ice cream with peanut and chocolate flavored sauce and chocolate-covered peanuts (chunks) added to the mix. Chai High consists of a vanilla base with the addition of a spicy tea flavoured sauce. Both flavours were tested with focus groups and thoroughly researched before they were brought to the market. These specialty ice creams are budgeted to sell at a 7% (Moose Madness) and 20% (Chai High) premium over the vanilla flavoured product.

BLAME IT ON TECHNOLOGY

It is time to review the results of Bakerview Dairies' diversification strategy. While the planning team's strategy appeared to be feasible, TJ is eager to see the actual figures for each quarter. It is Pat's responsibility to ensure that the appropriate reports are prepared for an accurate performance evaluation of the ice cream division's operations. TJ is expecting the third quarter reports on his desk by tomorrow but the computer system will not produce the necessary reports.

"That new ERP[1] system was supposed to streamline all of our processes and make my job easier," Pat thought. "Now I can't even get a manufacturing statement to print."

> *"That new ERP system was supposed to streamline all of our processes…..Now I can't even get a manufacturing statement to print."*

The ERP system was implemented in the ice cream division the previous quarter. While its automation was welcomed by almost everyone in the division, the new technology has come with a price. The ERP package includes a complex modeling language used to format the reports and financial statements. In addition, the general ledger accounts had to be correctly coded in order to properly display the accounts on the reports.

Pat had passed on the responsibility of coding the general ledger accounts and modeling the financial statements to her junior accounting clerk. She had intentions of assisting the clerk with the setup but never could find a spare moment in her busy schedule. The clerk did not have the experience to properly set up the accounts or statements, but attempted to do so, with disappointing results. (See Table 1.)

---

[1] ERP is an acronym for "enterprise resource planning." It is a software suite that automates the business processes of an organization.

Table 1

BAKERVIEW DAIRIES		
COWLIX ICE CREAM DIVISION		
Operating Income - For the Quarter Ended September 30		
Sales in litres		385,000
Net sales		$1,615,075
Cost of sales		
Advertising and promotion	$16,225	
Commissions	39,078	
Computer and supplies (production scheduling)	80,850	
Delivery, shipping and warehouse	12,925	
Direct labour	87,780	
Plant utilities	38,775	
Equipment maintenance	33,825	
Ingredients purchases	675,675	
Interest and bank charges	12,513	
Packaging	65,450	
Plant equipment amortization	67,650	
Plant lease	85,800	
Professional fees	7,975	
Quality control	40,425	
Research & development	48,400	
Administrative salaries	119,323	
Plant salary and wages (indirect)	56,415	
Gross margin		1,489,084
Miscellaneous administrative expenses	$ 3,255	
Administrative computer services	8,570	11,825
Operating Income		$ 114,166

While inventory levels for ingredients and ice cream have been stable for year end reporting purposes, it is important that seasonal changes are reflected on the interim financial reports. The accounting clerk has not customized the interim financial statements to show beginning and ending inventories for ingredients and finished goods.[2] Pat has provided you with the following account balances as of September 30. (See Table 2.)

Table 2

Inventory	Balance, July 1	Balance, September 30
Ingredients	$ 52,670	$48,550
Ice cream inventory	$14,270	$11,000

[2]The company does not have a work in process inventory. The batch process is complete when ice cream is packaged and hardened. This process is normally completed at the end of each day.

BEING PROACTIVE

According to the agenda, Monday morning's meeting is to start with an assessment of the profit margins for Bakerview Dairies' ice cream division. Based on the results, Pat anticipates a discussion on how these margins could be improved. Most notable is the Vanilla ice cream product line. While this flavour shows the highest volume of sales, the report shows its gross margin to be the lowest at 17%. Although this appears to be favourable for Vanilla when compared to the budgeted gross margin, management wants to improve this increase in gross margin. (See Table 3.)

Table 3

Bakerview Dairies YTD Income Statement (Partial) For Three Quarters Ended September 30				
	Vanilla	Moose Madness	Chai High	Total
Litre Sales	525,000	346,500	178,500	1,050,000
Sales	$2,131,459	$1,491,889	$ 781,403	$4,404,751
Cost of Sales	1,767,388	1,190,943	565,169	3,523,500
Gross Margin	$ 364,071	$ 300,946	$ 216,234	$ 881,251
Gross Margin (%)	17%	20%	28%	20%

"(Pat) is eager to be prepared to quickly determine the effect of each suggested action on the profits of the division."

One of the objectives of the meeting is to develop a list of actions that can be taken during the fourth quarter to increase the income of the division for that quarter. Pat is quite certain that the contribution margin per unit for Vanilla, Moose Madness and Chai High will still be $1.53, $1.78, and $2.47 respectively. She is also certain that Vanilla ice cream will sell at the budgeted price of $3.96 during this period. She is eager to be prepared to quickly determine the effect of each suggested action on the profits of the division. This preparation would give immediate feedback to the planning team, thus reducing the implementation time of the selected action and the amount of time Pat will have to spend in meetings.

Some informal discussions with marketing and operations have provided Pat with the following four preliminary alternatives to improve the gross margins on Vanilla ice cream. While these alternatives may be biased towards the individual suggesting the action, they are at least a starting point for Pat's model.

- Al Haagen in Marketing is convinced that the reason for low profit margins is the lack of promotion. He reckons, "We're only selling to repeat customers. More consumers need to be aware of our premium Vanilla ice cream. It needs to be able to stand on its own like a specialty flavour instead of being considered only as a complement to pie and cake. A $30,000 flyer promotion in major community newspapers should increase our sales of Vanilla ice cream by 10%."

- Carly Sims in Production is very concerned about the rising costs of vanilla and sugar. She argues, "We've had some unexpected cost increases in the ingredients that we use to make our ice cream. Storms in Madagascar last year ruined the vanilla crops raising the cost of the premium vanilla that is used to make our ice cream. And sugar prices have risen because our major suppliers in Brazil are encouraged to sell their sugar to boost Brazil's ethanol business that makes fuel from sugar cane. We need to find cheaper sources of ingredients. I talked to Larry in purchasing, and he is able to find alternative sources for vanilla and sugar. If we go with these suppliers the cost of ingredients for Vanilla ice cream could be less, consequently reducing variable costs by 5%. My only concern is that we will not be using a premium grade vanilla. Al has told me that this may reduce our budgeted unit sales by 5%."

- TJ Conner is more concerned about price. He strongly feels that a decrease in the price would encourage retailers to pass that savings on to their customers and increase volume sales. He believes that the company's success depends on Vanilla ice cream and wants to increase operating income by $50,000 for the fourth quarter by lowering the price to encourage more sales. Based on the competition, he thinks that if the price is somewhere between $3.75 and $3.85, sales in units will increase by 20%. He is concerned about determining what price should be charged in order to achieve this goal.

- Pat wants to consider other alternatives that would improve the operating income of the company. She is convinced that a shift in sales that favours an ice cream flavour with higher profit margins would increase the company's operating income. Bakerview's records currently indicate that the existing high profit margin flavour is Chai High. Pat estimates that there should be a special campaign to promote the sale of Chai High to change the sales mix to 40% for Vanilla, 33% for Moose Madness and 27% for Chai High. (See Tables 4 and 5 for current sales figures.)

If the campaign is successful she feels that the total sales volume would remain fairly stable, as existing consumers of Vanilla would switch to Chai High. She wants to know the maximum amount she can spend on advertising to achieve this sales mix and earn an additional fourth quarter operating income of $10,000.

Table 4

Schedule 1 – ANNUAL SALES & PRODUCTION BUDGET (Litres)*					
	Quarter 1	Quarter 2	Quarter 3	Quarter 4	TOTAL
	*Litres to Produce/Sell				
Vanilla	160,000	164,000	180,000	160,000	664,000
Moose Madness	110,000	112,000	124,000	110,000	456,000
Chai High	63,000	64,000	70,000	63,000	260,000
TOTAL LITRES					1,380,000

*Because beginning and ending ingredients and finished goods inventories are stable, sales quantities equal production and purchases.

Table 5

Schedule 2 - SALES and PRODUCTION BUDGET (Dollars) For the year ending December 31						
	Selling Price per litre	Quarter 1	Quarter 2	Quarter 3	Quarter 4	TOTA
(see schedule 1 for litres sold/produced)		Revenue				
Vanilla	$ 3.96	$ 633,600	$ 649,440	$ 712,800	$ 633,600	$2,629,44
Moose Madness	$ 4.25	467,500	476,000	527,000	467,500	1,938,00
Chai High	$ 4.75	299,250	304,000	332,500	299,250	1,235,00
TOTAL SALES		$ 1,400,350	$ 1,429,440	$ 1,572,300	$ 1,400,350	$5,802,44

Using the report designed by the accounting clerk, Pat is able to prepare a statement of revenues and expenses for the Vanilla product line for the quarter ending September 30. (See Table 6.)

Table 6

Cowlix Ice Cream Division Revenues and Expenses - Quarter Ended September 30 VANILLA PRODUCT LINE	
Sales in Litres	175,000
Net Sales	710,486
Cost of Sales	
Advertising and Promotion	$ 7,375
Commissions	17,763
Computer and Supplies (production scheduling)	36,750
Delivery, Shipping and Warehouse	5,875
Direct Labour	41,625
Plant Utilities	17,625
Equipment Maintenance	15,375
Ingredients Purchases	308,968
Interest and Bank Charges	5,688
Packaging	29,750
Plant Equipment Amortization	30,750
Plant Lease	39,000
Professional Fees	3,625
Quality Control	18,375
Research & Development	22,000
Administrative Salaries	54,237
Plant Salary and Wages (indirect)	28,875
Gross Margin	$ 26,830
Miscellaneous Administrative Expenses	1,480
Administrative Computer Services	3,895
Operating Income	$ **21,455**

YOU ARE IN CONTROL

The management accountant's job is to support managers by providing information on the organization's ability to meet its goals. It is the feedback that informs management of any controlling action that should be taken to ensure that planned targets are being met. This information must be presented in a readable format that assists in decision making.

As a management accountant for Bakerview Dairies your assignment is to assist Pat Duco in providing relevant and accurate information for the quarterly meeting with TJ Conner.

Activity 1   Produce a proper cost of goods manufacturing schedule and income statement for the ice cream division for the quarter ended September 30.

Activity 2   Assess Al Haagen's suggestion to develop an advertising campaign promoting Vanilla ice cream by comparing this alternative with the current situation. (Base your analysis on Vanilla ice cream.) Do you think this is the best way for the company to increase profits? Why or why not?

Activity 3   Assess Carly Sims' suggestion to find lower priced sources of vanilla and sugar. What effect will this suggestion have on operating income for the company? What other factors should be taken into consideration?

Activity 4   Assess TJ Conner's suggestion to lower the price of Vanilla ice cream. Determine the price to be charged to achieve the desired increase in operating income. Do you have any concerns about this approach?

Activity 5   Assess Pat Duco's suggestion to encourage more sales of Chai High ice cream by introducing an advertising campaign designed to change the sales mix of all flavours. Do you agree with her? What concerns do you have about changing the sales mix weight in favour of Chai High?

Activity 6   Which alternative has the most merit? Remember to consider the effect on income as well as the immediate and long term qualitative effects.

Bakerview Dairies

Module 3
Focus on Activities

The emphasis of this module is on activity based costing and activity based management.

At the end of this module you should be able to:
- Explain the importance of identifying appropriate cost drivers.
- Perform a regression analysis or identify situations where a regression analysis should be used to identify an appropriate cost driver.
- Identify situations where an organization would implement an Activity Based Costing system.
- Create activity pools to capture overhead costs, use appropriate activity drivers to allocate the activity costs to individual products.
- Compare the gross margins of individual products resulting from the use of activity based costing to the gross margins computed using traditional costing approach.
- Using the activity based approach, suggest ways to reduce the consumption of resources and thereby costs.
- Discuss the behavioural impact of costing systems.

T H E   P R O B L E M …

"While their profits seemed reasonable, (TJ) is concerned about product line gross margins."

It is Monday morning and TJ Conner is meeting with Al Haagen (Marketing Manager), and Pat Duco (Controller). TJ is concerned about recent financial trends and has called a meeting to review the current costing procedures for the ice cream division. While their profits seem reasonable, he is concerned about product line gross margins. Vanilla ice cream, which is their top selling frozen dairy product, shows the lowest margin. (See Table 1.) TJ wanted to know why. After discussing the issues at some length, Pat agreed that further investigation would be required.

Table 1: Partial Income Statement

BAKERVIEW DAIRIES - COWLIX ICE CREAM DIVISION PARTIAL INCOME STATEMENT FOR YEAR ENDED DECEMBER 31				
	VANILLA	**MOOSE MADNESS**	**CHAI HIGH**	**TOTAL**
Litre sales	700,000	466,667	233,333	1,400,000
Sales	$2,821,000	$1,989,000	$1,063,000	$5,873,000
Ingredients costs	$1,212,330	$855,872	$388,476	$2,456,678
Packaging	119,000	79,333	39,667	238,000
Direct labour	159,600	106,400	53,200	319,200
Overhead	829,400	553,300	276,100	1,658,800
Total manufacturing costs	$2,320,330	$1,594,905	$757,443	$4,672,678
Gross margin	$500,670	$394,095	$305,557	$1,200,322
Gross margin %	18%	20%	29%	20%

Specialty Flavours

Bakerview Dairies' Cowlix ice cream division has been producing ice cream for over a decade. Their product is well known for richness and taste which the owners attribute to premium ingredients and quality production processes. Each premium flavour requires specialized equipment. Moose Madness is chocolate ice cream with a peanut and chocolate flavoured sauce and chocolate-covered peanuts (chunks) added to the mix. Chai High consists of a vanilla base with the addition of a spicy tea flavoured sauce. Adding chunks to Moose Madness and flavoured sauces both require additional equipment. (See Table 5.) The chocolate covered peanut chunks are added to the Moose Madness flavour by a machine called the 'chunk feeder.' This process takes place after the vanilla flavour is added in the mix tank and the ice cream mix has been cooled to -6° C. The special sauces which are added to both flavours are 'swirled' into the ice cream using a machine called a 'variegator.' This process takes place just before the ice cream is packaged.

STATUS QUO

Jared Benot, the Operations Manager, is concerned about a number of changes that are taking place in the company.

- Before Bakerview's ice cream division had ventured into new flavours, they had just produced Vanilla ice cream. The manufacturing process was less complicated because they only had to purchase ingredients and schedule production runs for one flavour.

"They have had to deal with more issues since adding specialty flavours."

- They have had to deal with more issues since adding specialty flavours. Initially, additional equipment had to be purchased and added to production lines. Once production began, more time had to be scheduled to set up the chunk feeder for Moose Madness and the variegator for both specialty flavours. Scheduling production runs is now challenging, because specialty flavours take longer to produce. They also have to make sure that the production line is properly sterilized after a batch of Moose Madness to ensure that no residual peanuts are left in the line. While their ingredients labels warn of 'traces of nuts,' they want to avoid any legal hassles.

- Last year TJ purchased a new computer system to help streamline the business processes. The ERP[1] software was supposed to help with inventory availability, staffing and production scheduling. They have not seen all of the benefits yet as they are spending a lot of time on scheduling activities and purchasing.

- Al has been talking about adding more flavours in the near future. While Jared is excited about the opportunity to expand operations, he

---

[1]ERP is an acronym for "enterprise resource planning." It is a software suite which automates the business processes of an organization.

is also concerned about the increased complexity and burden on production lines and staff.

Ice Cream Production

Ice cream is produced in batches of 4000 litres. Each batch produces only one flavour and a batch takes between 17 and 24 hours from mixing to the packaged and frozen final product. The major task is preparing and mixing the ice cream. This requires the scientific expertise of Barney Larouche, who is the 'Mix Master.' Most of the production line consists of giant vats that blend and cool the product. The final task of the specialty products is the setup and running of the chunk feeder and variegator machines. Filling cartons, packaging and freezing is an automated process.

Bakerview's production process consists of a bill of materials that lists the cost and quantity of ingredients. Based on the fat content of the milk, the bill of materials can be adjusted and approved for each run. Information to calculate labour expenses for each batch is recorded on a routing sheet. This sheet also lists the sequence of processing steps for each station in production.

ALLOCATION OF OVERHEAD

The Bakerview Dairies' ice cream division uses a process costing system[2] to record ice cream production costs. Not all overhead costs are incurred evenly throughout the year. Therefore, to simplify the allocation of costs, a predetermined application rate is used to charge overhead to the product. The rate is based on estimated overhead costs and estimated direct labour dollar. Using this rate, overhead is applied to the product based on actual direct labour dollar.

When setting the current year's master budget, the planning committee had estimated that manufacturing overhead would be $1,656,146 and direct labour costs would be $307,490 (See Schedule 6, Module 1 Appendix). Any over- or under-allocated overhead is applied at year end directly to each product line based on actual direct labour dollar for the year.

When the committee reviewed the actual year end figures (Table 1) it is noted that direct labour costs have increased from the budgeted amount. The increase is mostly due to the higher demand for skilled tradespeople. As a result, quarterly product costing is incorrect, resulting in incorrect pricing that could eventually have an impact on future consumer demand.

---

[2]To reduce complexity in the case study, process costing is used. A batch system, such as ice cream production would normally use an operational costing system which is a hybrid of process and job costing.

ACTIVITY BASED COSTS ANALYSIS

Something has to be done about the costing problems. While the Vanilla ice cream product line does not appear to be as profitable as the others, Pat feels that the reports do not tell the entire story. The production of Vanilla ice cream consists of fewer steps than the other flavours, yet the profit margins are lower. Is this due to the costing process or the selling price? Pat has decided that an activity based approach to costing will present a more accurate picture of how costs should be allocated.

To allocate expenses based on activities, Pat first identifies eight categories of indirect expenses that are currently being allocated to ice cream production. (See Table 2.)

Table 2: Indirect Expenses for the current

Description	Amount
Plant utilities	$ 141,000
Salary and Wages (Indirect)	219,800
Computer and Supplies	294,000
Plant & Equipment Depreciation	246,000
Quality Control	147,000
Equipment Maintenance	123,000
Research & Development	176,000
Plant Lease	312,000
TOTAL	$1,658,800

To begin the activity based analysis Pat decided to observe the manufacturing activities, interview the personnel involved in the operations and map out the activities that consume the overhead resources. Based on her findings, Pat has identified the following activity pools:

- Scheduling production runs
- Machine setup
- Product administration
- Running machines
- Inspection
- Research and Development

Pat was not sure how to account for the plant lease.

Based on her discussions with the production manager regarding indirect labour, Pat has understood that two main activities account for their indirect labour consumption:

- 45% of indirect labour is necessary for cleaning, preparing and setting up equipment for batch runs.

- 55% of indirect labour is used to schedule production runs. This includes purchasing and releasing materials for production and scheduling production.

Setup time for batches of Vanilla ice cream is the shortest at about one hour. The setup for Chai High takes longer (about three hours) because the variegator equipment has to be set up and tested. The setup for Moose Madness takes the longest (about four hours) because both the variegator and chunk feeder machines have to be set up and tested. In addition, the equipment has to be thoroughly sterilized after a batch of Moose Madness in order to eliminate any residual peanuts from the system. (See Table 4.)

Quality control is responsible for ensuring that the finished product achieves strict standards set out by the ice cream mix master. Depending on the flavour being made, inspections are made at different stages of the process. Because it has no special additions, Vanilla ice cream is tested only at the mix stage and at the finished stage. In addition to these inspections, Chai High and Moose Madness are also inspected after the variegator stage of the process (see Table 4). All lab testing, labour, and supplies are traditionally allocated to the Quality Control account.

Next, the expenses allocated to computers and supplies are reviewed[3]. After interviewing the systems administrator, it is discovered that most of the computer's time and software expense is used to schedule production runs in the factory and to order and pay for the materials required in each production run (approximately 80%). The remaining 20% of computer expense is allocated to keeping records of the three products and their production.

Research and development activities are currently concentrated on reducing the fat content yet maintaining the flavour and consistency of the ice cream. Approximately 1050 hours have been spent on researching a variety of emulsifiers that could possibly achieve this goal. The goal of this research is to sell more of their specialty variety of ice creams. The marketing manager believes that this will not have an effect on Vanilla ice cream as many people perceive vanilla to contain fewer calories. Approximately equal amounts of time have been spent on each specialty product in this department.

---

[3]Computer and supplies costs relating to production scheduling and product administration are classified as manufacturing overhead. Those costs relating to general administrative work have already been allocated to 'Admin. computer services.' (See Module 1, Appendix, Schedule 8.)

Table 3: Equipment Maintenance Costs

Month	Equipment Maintenance	Labour Hours	Machine Hours
January	$ 8,700	97	492
February	9,600	98	535
March	10,100	97	574
April	10,200	94	570
May	11,300	101	645
June	11,200	104	566
July	11,400	97	656
August	10,300	102	566
September	10,000	92	574
October	10,300	100	594
November	10,500	106	578
December	9,400	93	535
Total	$123,000	1181	6885

While most of the overhead cost drivers are easy to identify, Pat is not sure how equipment maintenance costs should be allocated. Popular theory is split between using labour hours and machine hours. While she is able to gather some historical data (Table 3), she is unsure how it should be analyzed.

Plant utilities and plant equipment amortization are incurred to supply machine time to produce ice cream. The machines have a practical capacity of 8600 hours of productive time that can be supplied to ice cream production. Currently the plant is operating at 80% of capacity.

Table 4 summarizes the ice cream division's production activities and costs.

Table 4: Production Activities and Costs

Direct Costs and Activity Cost Drivers	Vanilla	Moose Madness	Chai High	Total
Production sales volume (litres)	700,000	466,667	233,333	1,400,000
Batch size (litres)	4000	4000	4000	
Direct labour hour per batch	27.2	27.2	27.2	
Machine hours per batch	17	24	19	
No. of annual production runs	175	117	58	350
No. of inspections per batch	2	3	3	
Setup time/run (hours)	1	4	3	
Number of product lines	1	1	1	
Research and Development hours		525	525	1050

Accurate recording systems provide details that reflect the actual costs required to manufacture products. This is especially true in organizations that provide multiple products or services. The management accountant should avoid using averages that smooth costs uniformly across all products. As a managerial accountant you will assess Bakerview Dairies' current costing system.

Activity 1

Determine the effectiveness of the current manufacturing overhead application process. By using the current overhead application rate will overhead be overstated or understated before the year end adjustment? By how much? What effect will this have on decisions that are made during the year? Could this affect the prices charged for the product?

Activity 2

Select an appropriate cost driver for equipment maintenance: Costs should be allocated based on the activity that drives the total cost. While in some cases this is easy to determine, in others it may be necessary to use regression analysis to find the activity that drives costs. Perform a regression analysis to determine the appropriate driver for Bakerview Dairies' equipment maintenance costs. Determine each driver's economic plausibility, goodness of fit and significance. Which is the appropriate cost driver? Provide your rationale.

Regression Analysis: A simple regression analysis can be performed manually or using a software spreadsheet. Steps to perform a regression analysis using Excel are given in the appendix of this module. In regression analysis the goodness of fit or R squared value explains how much of the change in equipment maintenance costs is explained by the independent variable.
Goodness of fit or R Square explains how much of the change in cost is explained by the independent variable. In the Bakerview Dairies' case, direct labour hours and machine hours are the two independent variables. Test each independent variable against maintenance costs to determine which drives machine costs better.

Significance of the independent variable may be established in terms of the computed t-value. Although certain factors such as sample size and variability of the data affect the reliability of the results, the rule of thumb for accepting the cost driver as significant, when the number of sample observations is 12 and a confidence level is 95%, is an absolute computed t-value or t stat of 2.2 or higher.

Activity 3

Allocate overhead costs to the products using activity based costing: The purpose of activity based costing is to allocate costs to activities within the organization and provide information that more accurately reflects actual costs. For Bakerview Dairies you will redistribute all of the indirect costs (Table 2) to the products by using activity based costing. Redraft the partial income statement using activity based costing. Use the activities that Pat has suggested. You may find the following template useful in presenting the financial statement.

	VANILLA	MOOSE MADNESS	CHAI HIGH	Facility Sustaining Cost	TOTAL
BAKERVIEW DAIRIES - COWLIX ICE CREAM DIVISION					
FOR YEAR ENDED DECEMBER 31					
Litre Sales	700,000	466,667	233,333		1,400,000
Sales	$2,821,000	$1,989,000	$1,063,000		$5,873,000
Manufacturing Costs					
Direct Manufacturing Costs					
Ingredients costs	1,212,330	855,872	388,476		$2,456,678
Packaging	119,000	79,333	39,667		238,000
Direct labour	159,600	106,400	53,200		319,200
Total Direct Costs					
Manufacturing Overhead					
Scheduling production runs					
Machine setup					
Product administration					
Running machines					
Inspection					
Research & Development					
Plant lease (facility sustaining cost)					
Total Manufacturing Overhead Costs					
Total Manufacturing Costs					
Gross Margin					
Gross Margin %					

Provide reasons that are specific to Bakerview Dairies' ice cream division why an activity based costing system may provide more appropriate cost allocations. Your answer should include rational proof to back your position including computations. Does this system cost the product more accurately? What are some of the behavioural concerns of changing from a traditional costing system to an activity based costing system? How would you overcome these issues?

Activity 4

Deal with management concerns: Jared Benot (Operations Manager) is concerned about gross profit margins of the Moose Madness and Chai High flavours after performing an activity based costing analysis of all three product lines. Review the income statement you have created using activity based costing. Identify what can be done to increase the profits of these two products.

Bakerview Dairies – Module 3

A P P E N D I X : I C E C R E A M P R O C E S S I N G

Table 5: Ice Cream Processing

APPENDIX: REGRESSION ANALYSIS IN EXCEL

Build a table in Excel listing the X and Y variables in columns. After building the table:

- Select TOOLS from the menu and then DATA ANALYSIS.

  If the 'DATA ANALYSIS' option is not available on the TOOLS menu:
  - Select ADD-INS on the TOOLS menu.
  - Click on the 'ANALYSIS TOOLPAK check box.
  - Click on the OK button.

- The Data Analysis scroll box will appear.

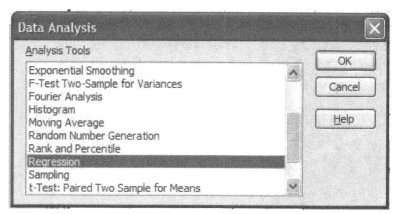

- Scroll down and select 'Regression' and input data as follows:

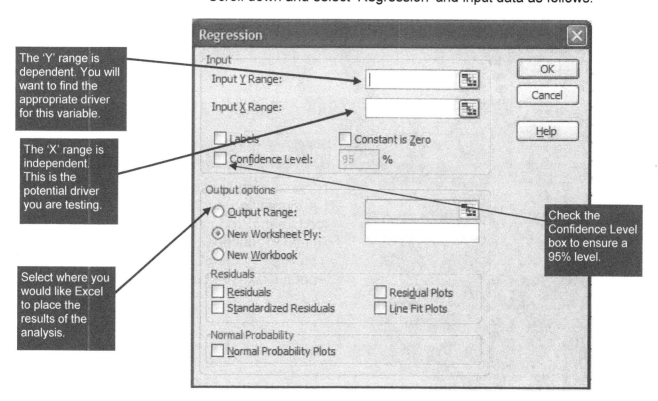

The 'Y' range is dependent. You will want to find the appropriate driver for this variable.

The 'X' range is independent. This is the potential driver you are testing.

Select where you would like Excel to place the results of the analysis.

Check the Confidence Level box to ensure a 95% level.

Bakerview Dairies

Module 4
Assessing Feedback

EMPHASIS AND OUTCOMES

The emphasis of this module is on master budgets and variance analysis.

At the end of this module you should be able to:
- Explain the importance of master budgets and standard costing when assessing performance.
- Prepare a static budget and a flexible budget using the activity based approach.
- Compute the flexible budget variance for revenue and each resource identified in the income statement using the activity based approach.
- Perform price and efficiency variance analysis on manufacturing costs.
- Explain the underlying reasons for price and efficiency variances.
- Discuss the importance of responsibility accounting when assessing feedback.

PERFORMANCE FEEDBACK

"Innovation comes with a price. Now we need to change our standard costing reports to reflect the new activity based approach to costing our product lines."

Pat Duco, controller for Bakerview Dairies, is on the phone with Carly Sims in production. Carly wants to review the year end reports for production. However Pat has not had a chance to create automated reports that reflect the new activity based costing system.

"A report of production variances is crucial to determining the ability of the plant to produce to standards."

"No Carly, we aren't going back to the old way of costing. We have determined that the gross margins reported using the old costing system are incorrect. The new activity based costing system allocates costs more accurately to each flavour we produce. These new reports should help with proper costing and pricing of our products. In addition it will also provide you with feedback on plant operations........I know you need this information as soon as possible.......by tomorrow?.......sure, I can have a variance analysis on the Vanilla product line by tomorrow afternoon."

As Pat hangs up the phone, she knows it is going to be another late night. Carly has a point. A report of production variances is crucial to determining the ability of the plant to produce to standards. Carly relies on these reports not only to determine the effectiveness of operations but to provide performance feedback to her employees as well. For now, Vanilla is a critical focus. Performing an activity based analysis of operations indicates that Vanilla ice cream provides the highest margins for Bakerview Dairies' ice cream division. As well, this provides a good starting point for developing the new reports based on production activities.

Bakerview Dairies manufactures Vanilla ice cream using six ingredients; cream, sucrose, fluid milk, milk powder, vanilla and a mixture of stabilizer and emulsifier. Based on benchmark studies with other ice cream manufacturers and its present operations, Bakerview has carefully developed standards for both quality control and the cost of producing its ice cream. Standard costs are used to determine the ability of production departments to control resources. The budgeted amount of ingredients used to make Vanilla ice cream, the standard cost of each ingredient and the amount of each ingredient required for purchase are in the following table. (See Table 1.)

Table 1

BUDGETED TOTAL INGREDIENT USE - Vanilla For the year ended December 31				
	price	per	Vanilla Quantity	Cost
Annual litre sales			664,000	
Cream	$4.00	litre	106,240	$ 424,960
Sucrose	$0.65	litre	46,812	30,428
Stabilizer & emulsifier	$3.50	litre	1,992	6,972
Fluid milk	$58.20	hectolitre+	1,527	88,883
Milk powder	$5.30	kilogram	16,600	87,980
Vanilla	$70.00	litre	7,636	534,520
TOTAL COST OF INGREDIENTS				$1,173,743

+a hectolitre is equal to 100 litres

The production process involves several operations in which conversion costs and ingredients are added to the product. Ingredients are added at the beginning of each operation requiring the basic mix, sauces, and particulates. Direct labour costs are added evenly throughout the process and overhead costs are allocated evenly throughout the process. (See Table 2.)

Table 2

BUDGETED DIRECT LABOUR For the year ended December 31	Vanilla
Number of litres	664,000
Batch size (litres)	4,000
Number of batches	166
Labour hours per batch	27.50
Total labour hours	4,565
Total direct labour cost per hour	$ 32.41
TOTAL DIRECT LABOUR COST	$ 147,952

On completion of each production run, automated equipment packages the ice cream. The standard cost for each package is $0.17.

Manufacturing overhead costs are allocated to specific manufacturing activities. (See Table 3.)

Table 3

ABC ANALYSIS OF BUDGETED MANUFACTURING OVERHEAD COSTS For the year ended December 31	
	Vanilla
Production Scheduling	$163,200
Machine Setup Expense	19,946
Product Administration	18,267
Running Machines*	216,853
Inspection	57,307
Plant Lease (Facility Sustaining Cost)+	156,000
TOTAL OVERHEAD COSTS	**$631,573**

*This is a mixed cost consisting of $106,296 of amortization.
+Plant lease is allocated based on production for purposes of variance analysis.

Budgeted administrative costs allocated to Vanilla ice cream are listed in Table 4.

Table 4

Budgeted Administrative Costs For the year ended December 31 Vanilla Ice Cream	
Number of units	664,000
Variable costs	
Commissions	67,362
Delivery and shipping	22,614
Total variable costs	$ 89,977
Fixed administrative costs	$ 294,470

Setup costs are incurred for cleaning, preparing and setting up equipment for batch runs. These costs consist of indirect labour and are applied based on the setup times for each flavour. Budgeted setup costs, along with the budgeted number of batches are shown in Table 5.

Table 5

BUDGETED SETUP COSTS For the year ended December 31	
	Vanilla
Number of batches made (4000 litres per batch)	166
Setup hours per batch	1
Total setup hours	166
Setup costs per batch	$ 120.15
BATCH SETUP COSTS	$ 19,946

Quality control is responsible for ensuring the finished product achieves strict standards set out by the ice cream mix master. Depending on the flavour being made, inspections are made at different stages of the process. Each flavour requires varying amounts of quality control time. Because Vanilla has no special additions it is tested only at the mix stage and at the finished stage. Budgeted inspections and costs per batch are shown in Table 6.

Table 6

BUDGETED INSPECTION COSTS	
For the year ended December 31	
	Vanilla
Number of batches made (4000 litres per batch)	166
Inspections per batch	2
Total inspection hours	332
Inspection costs per batch	$ 172.61
TOTAL INSPECTION COSTS	$ 57,307

Budgeted sales and revenues for the year are shown in Table 7.

Table 7

BUDGETED SALES	
For the year ended December 31	
	Vanilla
Sales (litres)	664,000
Sales Revenues	$ 2,629,440

ACTUAL PRODUCTION

After organizing the standard cost reports, Pat is able to download the following actual data from the computer system. (See Tables 8–14.)

Table 8

ACTUAL INGREDIENT USE				
For the year ended December 31				
			Vanilla	
	price	per	Quantity	Cost
Annual litre sales			700,000	
Cream	$4.00	litre	115,500	$ 462,000
Sucrose	$1.10	litre	49,350	54,285
Stabilizer & emulsifier	$3.50	litre	3,150	11,025
Fluid milk	$58.20	hectolitre+	1,575	91,665
Milk powder	$5.30	kilogram	17,850	94,605
Vanilla	$75.00	litre	6,650	498,750
TOTAL COST OF INGREDIENTS				**$1,212,330**
+a hectolitre is equal to 100 litres				

Table 9

ACTUAL DIRECT LABOUR For the year ended December 31	Vanilla
Number of litres	700,000
Batch size (litres)	4,000
Number of batches	175
Labour hours per batch	27.20
Total labour hours	4,760
Total direct labour cost per hour	$ 33.53
TOTAL DIRECT LABOUR COST (rounded)	$159,600

Table 10

ABC ANALYSIS OF ACTUAL MANUFACTURING OVERHEAD COSTS For the year ended December 31	Vanilla
Production scheduling	178,045
Machine setup expense	21,186
Product administration	19,600
Running machines*	220,370
Inspection (quality control)	58,800
Research & development	-
Plant lease (facility sustaining cost)+	156,000
TOTAL OVERHEAD COSTS	654,001

*This is a mixed cost consisting of $106,296 of amortization.

+Plant lease is allocated based on production for purposes of variance analysis.

Table 11

Actual Administrative Costs For the year ended December 31 Vanilla Ice Cream	
Number of units	700,000
Variable costs	
Commissions	71,014
Delivery and shipping	23,500
Total variable costs	$ 94,514
Fixed administrative costs	305,200

Table 12

ACTUAL INSPECTION COSTS For the year ended December 31	
	Vanilla
Number of batches made (4000 litres per batch)	175
Inspections per batch	2
Total inspection hours	350
Inspection costs per batch	$168.00
BATCH INSPECTION COSTS	$58,800

Table 13

ACTUAL SETUP COSTS For the year ended December 31	
	Vanilla
Number of batches made (4000 litres per batch)	175
Setup hours per batch	1.0
Total setup hours	175
Setup costs per batch	$121.06
BATCH SETUP COSTS	$21,186

Table 14

ACTUAL SALES For the year ended December 31	
	Vanilla
Sales (litres)	**700,000**
Sales Revenues	$ 2,821,000

Actual packaging costs were $119,000.

YOU ARE IN CONTROL

Budgets are a key component in planning and coordinating. A well constructed budget is a tool by which an organization can measure the success of the implementation of its strategies. The management accountant coordinates the development of the master budget and oversees the implementation of the processes that report actual activities and variances from budgeted activities. To be effective these variances should be communicated to the individual or team that is responsible for the control of the costs.

As a management accountant your assignment is to assist Pat Duco in effectively communicating the production department's ability to control the ice cream manufacturing process. Use Tables 1 through 14 to perform the following activities.

Activity 1

Prepare a static budget variance report for Vanilla ice cream by using an activity based income statement. What are the limitations of this report? What is the sales volume variance? You may find it helpful to use Table 15 provided in the appendix.

Activity 2

Prepare a flexible budget and compute the flexible budget and sales volume variances for Vanilla ice cream. You may find it helpful to use Table 16 provided in the appendix. What is the advantage of performing an analysis at this level?

Activity 3   For Vanilla ice cream, calculate the price and efficiency variances of the costs of:

- o   Direct labour
- o   Each of the ingredients

Determine at least one possible cause for each of the variances you have identified.

Activity 4   Based on the results of your variance analysis prepare a memo to Carly Sims in production explaining your key areas of concern. Who should be held responsible for these variances?

The following templates may be helpful in preparing the static and flexible variances in Activities 1 and 2.

Table 15

STATIC BUDGET VARIANCE REPORT – VANILLA ICE CREAM For the year ended December 31	Actual Results	Variance	F/UF	Static Budget
Units Sold				
Sales revenue	$	$		$
Unit-related costs				
Ingredients costs				
Cream	$	$		$
Sucrose				
Stablizer & emulsifier				
Fluid milk				
Milk powder				
Vanilla				
Total ingredients costs	$	$		$
Other unit-related costs				
Packaging	$	$		$
Direct labour				
Commissions				
Delivery & Shipping				
Total other unit-related costs	$	$		$
Batch-related costs				
Machine setup	$	$		$
Running machines				
Scheduling production runs				
Inspection				
Total batch-related costs	$	$		$
Product-related costs				
Research and Development	$	$		$
Product administration				
Total product-related costs	$	$		$
Facility-sustaining costs				
Plant equipment amortization	$	$		$
Plant lease				
Total facility-sustaining costs	$	$		$
Administrative costs	$	$		$
Total costs	$	$		$
OPERATING INCOME	$	$		$

[handwritten margin note:] Static Budget Compares Bdgt d/s with actual d/s

Table 16

| | | FLEXIBLE BUDGET VARIANCE REPORT – VANILLA ICE CREAM | | | | | |
| | | For the year ended December 31 | | | | | |
	Actual Results	Flexible Budget Variance	F/UF	Flexible Budget	Sales Volume Variance	F/UF	Static Budget
Units Sold							
Sales revenue	$	$		$	$		$
Unit-related costs							
Ingredients costs							
Cream	$	$		$	$		$
Sucrose							
Stablizer & emulsifier							
Fluid milk							
Milk powder							
Vanilla							
Total ingredients costs	$	$		$	$		$
Packaging	$	$		$	$		$
Direct labour							
Commissions							
Delivery & Shipping							
Total unit-related costs	$	$		$	$		$
Batch-related costs							
Machine setup	$	$		$	$		$
Running machines							
Scheduling production runs							
Inspection							
Total batch-related costs	$	$		$	$		$
Product-related costs							
Research and Development	$	$		$	$		$
Product administration							
Total product-related costs	$	$		$	$		$
Facility-sustaining costs							
Plant equipment amortization	$	$		$	$		$
Plant lease							
Total facility-sustaining costs	$	$		$	$		$
Administrative costs	$	$		$	$		$
Total costs	$	$		$	$		$
OPERATING INCOME	$	$		$	$		$

Actual dolars
Cost / unit

Bakerview Dairies

Module 5
Inventory and Income

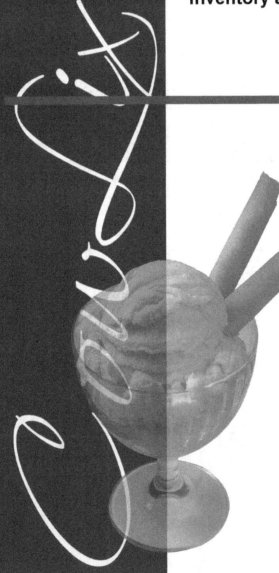

The emphasis of this module is on income statement preparation using absorption costing and variable costing approaches.

At the end of this module you should be able to:
- Explain the effects of using absorption and variable costing methods on income.
- Explain how inventory costing methods can influence management decisions.
- Prepare income statements using absorption and variable costing approaches.

A CLOSER LOOK AT INCOME

'What effect will this have on income...?"

This question is an inevitable topic at almost every meeting Pat attends. Naturally, profitability is a focus of all planning decisions that are made in the ice cream division of Bakerview Dairies. Therefore it is important that the financial statements accurately reflect the income of the division.

"Naturally, profitability is a focus of all planning decisions that are made in the ice cream division of Bakerview Dairies."

Pat is also aware of the importance of financial statements in assessing performance. The company focuses its efforts on the production department's ability to maximize quality and control costs. She is concerned that as costs increase, pressure may be placed on production to manipulate scheduling to reduce short term costs and increase the reported income by stockpiling inventories. This can happen if the absorption costing method is used for inventory reporting. Beginning and ending finished ice cream inventory for the year are both 1000 litres. The inventories have always been reported at standard costs which have not been adjusted in the past. However, as there is a potential for cost increase, Pat is aware that she should assess the current method of reporting inventories.

As a starting point she tells you that revenues for Vanilla ice cream were $2,821,000 for the current period and that the ice cream division uses standard costing. Currently, income statements are prepared using the traditional approach. Then she provides you with the current period's actual costs and standard costs. (See Tables 1 and 2.)

Table 1

Actual Costs For the year ended December 31 Vanilla Ice Cream		
Number of litres		700,000
Variable costs		
Ingredients	$	1,212,330
Direct labour		159,600
Packaging costs		119,000
Indirect manufacturing costs		372,105
Manufacturing costs	$	1,863,035
Commissions		71,014
Delivery and shipping		23,500
Administrative costs		94,514
Total variable costs	$	1,957,549
Fixed costs		
Manufacturing costs		281,896
Administrative costs		305,200
Total fixed costs	$	587,096

Table 2

Standard Costs For the year ended December 31 Vanilla Ice Cream		
Number of litres		664,000
Variable costs		
Ingredients	$	1,173,743
Direct labour		147,952
Packaging costs		112,880
Indirect manufacturing costs		351,010
Manufacturing costs	$	1,785,585
Commissions	$	67,362
Delivery and shipping		22,614
Administrative costs	$	89,976
Total variable costs	$	1,875,561
Fixed costs		
Manufacturing costs	$	280,563
Administrative costs		294,470
Total fixed costs	$	575,033

The method in which inventories are costed can affect the operating income of a manufacturing organization. The costing choice may also have an effect on the behaviour of managers responsible for production. As a management accountant your task is to ensure that inventory costing fairly reflects the financial position of the ice cream division.

Activity 1

Address Pat's concern about inventory costing by preparing a traditional income statement for Vanilla ice cream using the variable costing method. For analysis purposes assume that the ending inventory is 5000 litres instead of 1000. What effect will this method of reporting have on operating income?

Activity 2

Address Pat's concern about inventory costing by preparing a traditional income statement for Vanilla ice cream using the absorption costing method. As in Activity 1, for analysis purposes assume that the ending inventory is 5000 litres instead of 1000. What effect will this method of reporting have on operating income?

Activity 3

Prepare a memo to Pat Duco explaining the difference between variable costing and absorption costing. Which method should she use to address the concerns about inventory costing? How should Pat ensure that ethical measures are taken when reporting inventory costs?

Bakerview Dairies

Module 6
Allocating Resources

The emphasis of this module is on the importance of using relevant information in decision making and on managing limited resources with a view to maximize profit.

At the end of this module you should be able to:
- Maximize the total contribution margin and allocate resources using linear programming.
- Explain the importance of considering both qualitative and quantitative factors when making a decision.
- Determine which costs are relevant when making decisions.
- Analyze special sales order requests and make appropriate decisions.
- Analyze outsourcing decisions.

T H E   D I S A G R E E M E N T   A N D   T H E   S O L U T I O N ...

The development of the activity based costing approach has created added enthusiasm in the ice cream division of Bakerview Diaries. TJ calls Pat into his office for a meeting. Jared (Operations) and Carly (Production) are discussing the ice cream manufacturing process. They have different opinions on how they will maximize their production efforts.

"It is April and the operations team is gearing up for the summer months when sales are at the highest level of the year."

It is April and the operations team is gearing up for the summer months when sales are at the highest level of the year. The production department prepares for these months by increasing the number of batches produced in May, June and July. During the fall and winter months, the normal production is one batch of ice cream per day, four days a week. However, during the peak months, they usually produce one batch a day, seven days a week. Each batch consists of 4000 litres of ice cream and is usually shipped within two days to customers. Since Vanilla is one of their best sellers, they want to ensure that at least 15 batches of Vanilla ice cream are produced per month.

Where possible, resources are utilized to maximize profits; however, they are bound by the labour and equipment restrictions. Equipment usage is limited to 24 hours per day, 7 days per week. With current staff levels, labour is restricted to 900 hours per month. Each ice cream flavour requires varying amounts of these resources as follows:

Table 1

MACHINE AND LABOUR REQUIREMENTS PER BATCH				
	Vanilla	Moose Madness	Chai High	Maximum Available per month
Machine Hours	17	24	19	720 hours
Labour Hours	27.5	27.5	27.5	900 hours

Cream is one of the major ingredients of Cowlix ice cream. The main purpose for creating the ice cream division was to make efficient use of the cream that is taken from the raw milk in the milk processing division. In the milk processing division, each hectolitre (100 litres) of milk has five percent of the cream skimmed at the separation stage of the production line. The skimmed milk is then pasteurized, homogenized and eventually bottled in the milk processing division (Figure 6, Appendix). The cream is transferred to the ice cream division.

The cream skimmed from milk in the milk processing division is the most inexpensive source of cream for the ice cream division. Purchasing it from outside suppliers would cost more per litre; not to mention the additional overhead for purchasing. As a result, ice cream production is limited to the cream that is skimmed from the milk processed in the milk processing division. Larry, in Operations, anticipates that the milk processing division will purchase 4,220 hectolitres of milk per month in the spring and summer months. After separating the cream and allowing for 0.25% shrinkage, there will be 21,000 litres of cream available per month for ice cream. A batch of Vanilla ice cream requires 640 litres of cream, while a batch of Moose Madness requires 500 litres and Chai High requires 540 litres.

This year there are additional constraints on ice cream production. Severe storms have pummeled Madagascar, the key vanilla-producing region in the world. Vanilla from this island off the east coast of Africa is said to be the best in the world and it is agreed that Bakerview's Cowlix vanilla flavour recipe is successful because of this prime flavouring. As a result, supplies of quality vanilla flavouring are restricted. Bakerview's supplier has already cautioned that shipments of vanilla may be limited to 1000 litres per month during their peak production months. Cowlix Vanilla ice cream requires 46 litres of vanilla flavouring per batch, while the Moose Madness and Chai High flavours each require 20 litres.

The only other restriction on processing is the special sauce for the production of the Chai High flavour. An importer in Vancouver is able to supply a maximum of 2000 litres of the sauce per month. One 4000 litre batch of Chai High requires 300 litres of mix.

"Jared and Carly are having a disagreement on how to optimize the production plan in order to maximize profit."

Jared and Carly are having a disagreement on how to optimize the production plan in order to maximize profit. Jared's opinion is that the restriction on the supply of cream from the milk processing division is limiting production of ice cream and consequently profit. Carly, on the other hand, argues that the lack of quality vanilla is causing profit reduction. Jared suggests that at extra expense, additional cream should be purchased from an outside source in order to maximize production and profits. Carly insists that the company needs to focus on sources and supplies of vanilla. The profit margin per batch of each flavour is provided in the following table:

Table 2

PROFIT MARGIN per BATCH	
Vanilla	$ 4,710
Moose Madness	$ 3,560
Chai High	$ 4,650

TJ wants to build a model to settle the disagreement and make suggestions on how the production line could optimize the production plan and maximize profits.

AN OPPORTUNITY

As soon as Pat returns to her office after her meeting with TJ, Al Haagen (Marketing) bursts through the door.

"I just spoke to the organizers of the Sun Ski Race. They want to purchase 20,000 litres of Vanilla ice cream to serve at all the functions and venues for their annual race and winter carnival next January. Many of the participants come from across Canada and are providing us with an excellent marketing opportunity. Production has idle capacity at that time of the year. This would allow us to make use of our resources.

"Production has idle capacity at that time of the year. This would allow us to make use of our resources."

The organizers have suggested that they would accept a price of $2.00 per litre and have agreed that we can place a full page advertisement in their programs for free and they will even absorb the delivery and shipping costs!"

Pat thinks for a moment, "Al, will that price cover all of our costs?"

"Well, our cost per litre of Vanilla is around $1.75 and the rest will cover shipping costs which should be around $1200. Any costs above that should be written off as advertising. You're the expert on the costs. I'll leave it to you to work out the details."

"Let me guess. You want this information by tomorrow, right?"

"I knew you could do it!"

"Sure," responds Pat sullenly as Al walks out the door. She clicks the mouse on her desktop organizer and adds another 'to do' item. When she is finished, she quickly pulls together costing information that will help get her started on Al's request. (See Table 3.)

Table 3

VANILLA ICE CREAM UNIT COSTING (per litre)	
INGREDIENTS	
Cream	$0.64
Sucrose	$0.05
Stabilizer & emulsifier	$0.01
Fluid milk	$0.13
Milk powder	$0.13
Vanilla	$0.81
TOTAL	$1.77

While the cost of ingredients is a good place to start, Pat needs to consider other relevant costs as well. The production of a 4000 litre batch of Vanilla ice cream requires 27.5 hours of direct labour at a cost of $32.41 per hour and packaging costs of $0.17 per litre. Setup costs to produce Vanilla amount to $120.15 per batch and running the machines costs $77 per hour. A batch of vanilla ice cream requires 17 hours of machine time to produce. Additionally, two quality control inspections take place for each batch run at a cost of $172.61 per inspection. There will be no commissions or delivery and shipping costs for this special order.

WHAT TO DO ABOUT PAYROLL

Before she leaves for the day, Pat has to deal with one more issue: payroll. Currently the company outsources payroll through a service provider who charges $150 per month to do the weekly payroll. Bakerview has hired a clerk to work two days a week to prepare and enter the data that will be used by the service provider to produce the payroll. She is paid $200 per day.

TJ's goal is to use the newly implemented ERP[1] system for all of their business processes. Using the service provider to perform the payroll function currently requires manual entry of the entire weekly wage and salary data into the ERP system to properly record product costs. TJ wants to sever ties with the service provider and streamline the operations by performing the payroll task on the new system.

The ERP system came with a fully operational payroll system. While Bakerview had originally paid $2500 for the payroll module, it still requires additional consulting time to customize the software to operate in Bakerview's environment. The consulting firm that originally implemented the software has recently provided a quote of $3540 for training; however the project coordinator has not yet sent a quote for implementation of the software.

---

[1]ERP is an acronym for "enterprise resource planning." It is a software suite which automates the business processes of an organization.

Pat estimates that the entry time will be reduced from two days to one day per week if they bring the payroll function in-house. However, Pat will have to consider the additional software cost to periodically update the government required information for payroll taxes and other deductions. The consulting firm has stated that they can update their current software contract to include semi-annual payroll updates for $500 per year. Pat would like to assess the costs based on three years of operations.

YOU ARE IN CONTROL

A management accountant must provide relevant and accurate information to assist in decision making. Often, this information is used by other managers in making decisions that affect the strategic direction of the company. When making decisions, the manager will have to take into account both the quantifiable data and the qualitative effects of the decision on the organization.

Activity 1

Analyze and assess the production resources to determine the optimal mix of ice cream production to maximize profits. To do this you will formulate and solve a linear programming model of Bakerview's ice cream division listing production constraints and use this model to answer the following questions:

- At the optimal solution, which constraints are binding? (Which resources have been totally used?) Whose assumptions about restrictions are correct, Jared's or Carly's? How do you know this?

- By adjusting the limitations on the model, which additional resources should they consider acquiring and at what additional cost?

If you choose to use the Solver tool in Excel to determine the optimal mix, the appendix provides guidelines to help build the model.

Activity 2

Consider the implications of accepting the special order to provide ice cream to the Sun Ski Race. Will this sale increase the company's income? If so, by how much? What qualitative factors should be considered for this decision?

Should Bakerview consider this special order even if it reduces income? Why or why not?

Prepare a memo to Al Haagen in Marketing discussing the effects of the special order on income.

Activity 3

Based on the information provided, what is the maximum amount that Bakerview's ice cream division should be willing to pay for implementation of the payroll software? Provide the rationale for your recommendation supported with calculations and qualitative factors you have taken into consideration. What are the pros and cons?

APPENDIX: USING SOLVER IN EXCEL

Linear Programming model:

You may wish to use the Solver tool in Excel to determine the optimal production mix. If you do, the following layout may be useful. (See Figure 1.) The data in the model is not relevant to this situation but provides you with an example to assist in understanding the components of the solution. Note those cells that require formulae, those which contain the optimal solution and those which require input data. (Do not include the text boxes labeled 'Target Cell' and 'By Changing Cells.' They are referenced on the next page. Formulae are provided in the footnotes.)

Target C●

Figure 1

	A	B	C	D	E	F	G
1		LINEAR PROGRAMMING MODEL LAYOUT					
2		Chocolate	Vanilla	Banana	Total Profit		
3	*Profit per litre*	$1.00	$0.90	$0.95	$0.00[2]		
4							
5	*Resource Constraints*	*Resources used per litre*			Litres Used		Litres Available
6	**Milk**	0.45	0.5	0.4	0.00[3]	<=	2000
7	**Sugar**	0.5	0.4	0.4	0.00	<=	1500
8	**Cream**	0.1	0.15	0.2	0.00	<=	600
9							
10	*Demand Constraints*						
11	**Min.litres of choc.**	500	0	0			
12	**Max.litres of Vanilla**	0	2000	0			
13							
14	*Decision Variables*						
15		Chocolate	Vanilla	Banana			
16	*Litres Produced*	0	0	0			
17							
18	Key to model	Cells with this shade require a formula		Solver will place the solution in cells with this shade		User input will be placed in these cells	

'By Changing Cells'

This model optimizes production of Chocolate, Vanilla and Banana ice cream in order to maximize profits. Cells G6 thru to G8 indicate a limited supply of milk, sugar and cream. Cells B11 and C12 indicate that the optimal solution must produce a minimum of 500 litres of chocolate and a maximum of 2000 litres of Vanilla.

---

[2] =(B3*B16)+(C3*C16)+(D3*D16)
[3] =(B6*B16)+(C6*C16)+(D6*D16)

After you have created the linear programming model use the Solver tool in Excel to optimize production. Access and use Solver using the following steps:

▪ From the menu bar select TOOLS and SOLVER.

If the 'SOLVER' option is not available on the TOOLS menu:
- Select ADD-INS on the TOOLS menu.
- Click on the 'SOLVER ADD-IN' check box.
- Click on the OK button.

▪ The 'Solver Parameters' dialogue box will appear. (See Figure 2. Note: at this point the dialogue box will appear without cell references.)

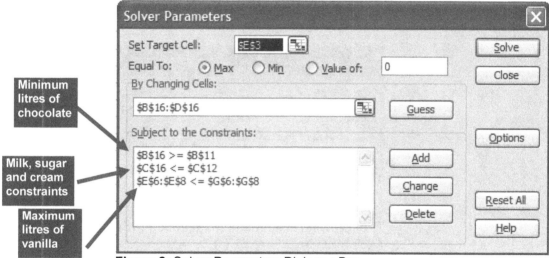

Figure 2: Solver Parameters Dialogue Box

- Select the 'Target Cell' on the model. This is the cell that will contain the total profit formula for the production mix. (See model on previous page.)

- Because you want to maximize profits, select the 'Max' radio button in the 'Equal To:' section.

- The 'By Changing Cells:' section should contain the cells where you want Solver to display the number of units to produce of each product. (See model on previous page.)

- The 'Subject to the Constraints:' section will contain the various dollar and resource constraint formulae for Solver to analyze. Use the 'Add' button to the right to add a constraint formula. The following dialogue box will appear. (See Figure 3.)

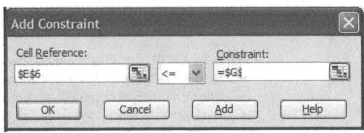

Figure 3

- The model on the previous page illustrates 'Cell Reference' and 'Constraints.' Example: To add the constraint that indicates that the optimal solution must have a minimum of 500 litres of Chocolate ice cream fill in the 'Add Constraint' dialogue box as shown in Figure 4.

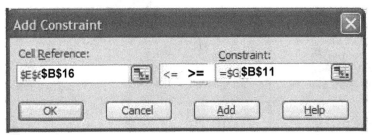

Figure 4

- When all parameters have been entered, select the 'Solve' button. The following dialogue box will appear. (See Figure 5.)

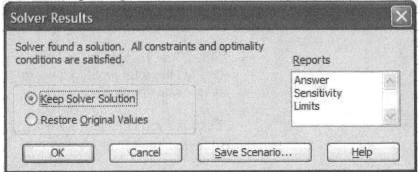

Figure 5

- Under the 'Report' selection box, select 'Answer' and 'Sensitivity.'

- Click the 'OK' button.

A P P E N D I X : M I L K   P R O C E S S I N G   D I V I S I O N

69

BAKERVIEW DAIRIES – PROCESSING OVERVIEW

**MILK PROCESSING
DIVISION**

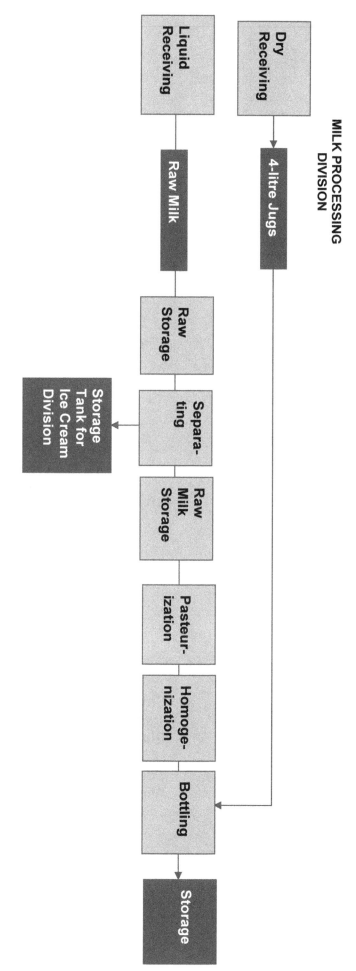

Figure 6

Bakerview Dairies

Module 7
Allocating Costs

EMPHASIS AND OUTCOMES

The emphasis of this module is on the allocation of support department costs to the operating departments and joint product costs to individual products.

At the end of this module you should be able to:
- Allocate the cost of a support department that provides service almost exclusively to operating departments using single-rate and dual-rate methods.
- Explain the qualitative effects of using budgeted and actual allocation rates to distribute support department costs to a cost or profit centre.
- Allocate the costs of support departments to operating departments using the direct and step down methods.
- Allocate the joint costs of resources incurred in the simultaneous production of multiple products using:
  - Sales Value at Splitoff Method
  - Physical Measure Method
  - Estimated Net Realizable Value (NRV) Method.
- Discuss the implications of using different joint cost allocation methods.

TWO DIVISIONS

Bakerview Dairies consists of two divisions; the milk processing division and the ice cream division. The ice cream division produces Bakerview's brand name Cowlix ice cream while the milk processing division produces a variety of fluid milk products in four-litre jugs. The information systems of both divisions operate separately from each other. However, some resources cross boundaries between divisions. This has always been controversial because the methods in which costs are allocated affect the profit margins of both divisions.

TJ Conner (President) and Pat Duco (Controller) are reviewing the cost allocation methods currently practised by the company. They want to implement a cost allocation method that fairly distributes costs between both divisions and, at the same time, motivates employees to use joint resources prudently. They want to focus on how the following costs will be allocated between the ice cream and milk processing divisions.
- Research and development costs
- Housekeeping costs
- Human resources costs

Another concern is the joint cost allocation of the cost of raw milk between skim milk that is processed in the milk processing division and the cream that is used in the ice cream division.

SHARING COSTS ...

Research & Development

Developing a marketable product is a continuing challenge for Bakerview Dairies. The demand for dairy products is influenced by media coverage of the latest nutritional findings. As consumers change their opinions about the content of food products, Bakerview's Research and Development department has to find ways to alleviate any negative effect on the consumer's perception of its products. This challenge is in addition to the task of producing a product that satisfies people's tastes and lifestyles.

Bakerview's ice cream division produces 'Cowlix Natural Ice Cream.' Many consumers like both the taste of Cowlix and the fact that the Cowlix brand's ingredients come from dairy cows that are given natural vitamin supplements instead of synthetic additives. The Research and Development department ensures that Cowlix ice cream contains a lower percentage of fat than the competitor's product.

"The company has realized that creating two separate research and development departments would not be cost effective."

The fluid milk processing division of Bakerview also relies on continuous research. The division's objective is to produce a natural product with high nutritional value. Various technologies to purify and homogenize milk are constantly being tested for the ability to provide a product that not only tastes good, but also is healthy with a long shelf life.

The company has realized that creating two separate Research and Development departments would not be cost effective. As a result it has created one department that services both divisions. Currently total research and development costs are allocated between the two divisions as: 75% to the ice cream division and 25% to the milk processing division. It has been argued that the ice cream division has three products while the milk processing division has only one; therefore the product has been considered as the cost driver. This method of allocation is now being questioned by the ice cream division personnel, whose performance evaluation is based on both productivity and cost. They argue that all three product lines in the ice cream division use the same equipment for most of the process. Therefore costing based on product lines unfairly increases costs for the ice cream division.

Both the milk processing division and the ice cream division are willing to explore changes to the method of costing. Pat feels that an allocation method based on hours of research and development used by each division is the best solution.

However she is uncertain whether the single-rate or the dual-rate allocation method should be used. She is also not clear as to whether the allocation is based on budgeted costs or actual costs.

As a starting point, she is considering two approaches:

- Pool all of the research and development costs (fixed and variable) into one pool and allocate based on one rate.

- Separate fixed and variable costs into cost pools and allocate using two separate rates.

She must also determine the appropriate allocation rate(s), the appropriate costs for the allocation and the usages (budgeted or actual).

Pat has gathered the following data (see Table 1) on research and development costs and hours.

Table 1

Budgeted Research & Development Costs				
	BUDGET	ACTUAL	VARIANCE	
Fixed Costs	$ 123,750	$ 125,000	$ 1,250	U
Variable Costs	116,250	109,667	6,583	F
TOTAL COSTS	$ 240,000	$ 234,667	$ 5,333	F

Research & Development Usage (hours)			
	BUDGET	ACTUAL	VARIANCE	
Milk processing division	256	355	99	U
Ice cream division	1050	910	140	F
TOTAL HOURS	1306	1265	41	F

Pat wants to choose a method that:
- fairly distributes costs to both divisions.
- motivates the Research and Development department manager to improve efficiency.
- assists all users of the Research and Development department with their short and long range plans.
- encourages a realistic estimation of costs.

Housekeeping and Human Resource Costs

Both the milk processing division and the ice cream division receive housekeeping and human resource services from within the company. While Bakerview Dairies does not keep specific accounts for these services, periodically Pat will allocate the appropriate administrative costs to these two pools. She then allocates these costs to each division in order to determine profitability. This analysis is performed on a regular basis using the direct method.

Pat would like to ensure that the direct method continues to fairly report the cost of these resources by the milk processing and ice cream divisions. She is considering the step down method as an alternative approach. The housekeeping costs are allocated based on floor space and the human resources costs are allocated based on the percentage of use. (See Table 2.)

Table 2

		Housekeeping	Human
Department	**Annual cost**	**(square feet of floor space)**	**Resources (% usage)**
Housekeeping	$48,000		5%
Human Resources	$60,000	1,000	
Milk Processing Division		64,000	50%
Ice Cream Division		35,000	45%
TOTAL	$108,000	100,000	100%

MILK VS. CREAM

TJ and Pat are also concerned about the way in which costs are recorded for the cream that is used in ice cream production. The cream, which is separated from the raw milk in the milk processing division (see Figure 1, Appendix), is costed at the current market value for cream. On several occasions in the past, Pat has indicated to TJ that as a result of this costing practice, the ice cream division's gross profit margins are understated. She insists that because raw milk only consists of 5% cream, the cost of the cream received from the milk processing division should only be 5% of the cost of the raw milk.

"Pat has indicated to TJ that as a result of this costing practice, the ice cream division's gross profit margins are understated."

Pat wants to address the joint cost allocation of raw milk between skim milk and cream. The milk processing division purchases raw (unprocessed) milk at the market price, which averages $58.20 per hectolitre in the current year. After allowing for 0.25%[1] shrinkage, 95% of the milk goes on to the pasteurization, homogenization and bottling stage. The sales value of the skim milk after the cream is separated and before processing is $0.60 per litre. The remaining 5% is cream, transferred to the ice cream division for production of ice cream. The value of the cream at this point is $4.02 per litre. Table 3 contains annual production and sales value figures.

[1] Shrinkage takes place when milk is unavoidably lost as it remains in pipelines, adheres to tanker walls and/or other plant equipment, and is washed away in the cleaning operations.

Table 3

ANNUAL RAW MILK PROCESSING							
		Yield at Splitoff (litres)		Final Production			
				Units		Price	Total
Raw Milk Purchased: (Hectolitres)	45,376.6	Liquid Skim	4,300,000	1,075,000	4-litre containers of skim milk	$3.60	$3,870,000
Cost of Raw Milk (Hectolitre)	$58.20	Cream	226,316	1,400,000	litres of ice cream	Various	$5,873,000
		Shrinkage	11,344				
Annual Cost of Raw Milk	$2,640,918						

Table 4 lists the costs that are incurred to purchase, store and process the raw milk to the separation stage.

Additional Joint Costs	
Storage	$132,000
Processing	264,000
Purchasing	26,000
	$ 422,000

Table 4: Costs to Purchase, Store and Process Raw Milk

In order to do a complete analysis of joint costing alternatives, Pat is aware that Bakerview Dairies' fluid milk division sells a four-litre container of skim milk for $3.60. The separable costs to complete and sell skim milk are $816,000 and the separable costs for ice cream are $3,613,347.

YOU ARE IN CONTROL

In business, costs play a key role in setting prices and measuring profitability. Prices and profitability are based on costs and performance is rewarded based on cost controls. Therefore accurate reporting of costs is essential for a business's success. Cost cutting measures in many organizations and the practice of responsibility accounting have created situations where unethical practices of managers have been observed. Managers may be tempted to find ways to reduce costs in the short term that have a negative effect on the long term financial position of the company. As such the allocation of costs is a challenge that every management accountant is likely to face.

As a management accountant you will help Pat assess the methods that Bakerview Dairies uses to allocate costs between the milk processing and ice cream divisions.

Activity 1

Review the options Pat is considering for the allocation of research and development costs. Choose the appropriate method and allocate the cost to both divisions.

Prepare a memo to Pat Duco with your recommendation.

| Activity 2 | Based on the costing data presented prepare an analysis of the three methodologies for allocation of joint costs between skim milk and cream: |

1. Sales Value at Splitoff Method
2. Physical Measure Method
3. Estimated Net Realizable Value (NRV) Method

In a memo to Pat discuss the following:

- In your opinion, which method of allocating joint costs should be chosen? Why?
- What are the implications of this choice:
  - for the ice cream division?
  - for the milk processing division?
- Why is this method preferred over the existing costing method?

| Activity 3 | - Determine the housekeeping and human resource cost pools that should be allocated to the milk processing and ice cream divisions using the direct allocation method.
- Now, ranking the housekeeping costs first and then the human resources costs, allocate the housekeeping and human resource cost pools to the milk processing and ice cream divisions using the step down allocation method.
- Which method provides a more accurate allocation methodology? Are there any merits in changing the allocation method? |

BAKERVIEW DAIRIES – PROCESSING OVERVIEW

**MILK PROCESSING
DIVISION**

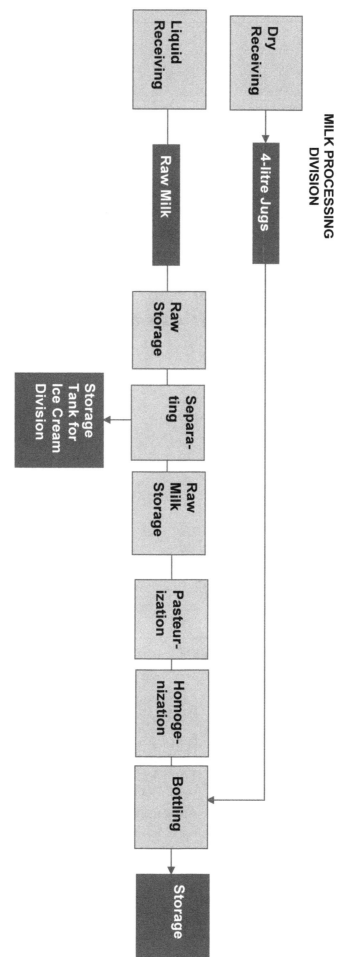

Figure 1

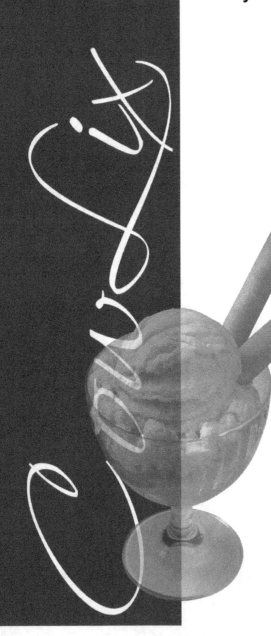

Bakerview Dairies

Module 8
Analyzing Costs and Profitability

EMPHASIS AND OUTCOMES

This module focuses on inventory management and customer profitability analysis.

At the end of this module you should be able to:
- Prepare and analyze the results of a customer profitability report.
- Apply the economic order quantity decision model in order to minimize inventory ordering and carrying costs.
- Identify additional constraints that should be taken into consideration when evaluating inventory costs.

CUSTOMERS – A CLOSER LOOK

Al Haagen (Marketing) is passionate about customers. As marketing manager and co-owner of Bakerview Dairies' ice cream division it is no surprise he has this attitude. However, Al goes beyond the means of many marketing managers to please his customers. In addition to regular on-site visits with purchasing agents of Bakerview's larger clients, he is often seen visiting the owners of many local small markets and restaurants that purchase Bakerview's Cowlix brand ice cream. His passion has reaped rewards as Bakerview's customer base for ice cream has grown locally over the past five years.

TJ Conner (president) is aware of Al's passion and encourages his desire to maintain a customer-centric outlook on the organization. However, he does not want Al to become 'customer obsessed.' TJ and Al are partners in Bakerview Dairies and both are proactive in managing the organization. Nevertheless TJ wants to ensure that Al's efforts are profitable. He calls a meeting with Al to discuss this issue.

"TJ Conner (president) is aware of Al's passion and encourages his desire to maintain a customer-centric outlook on the organization."

"I think our efforts in building the ice cream division have paid off," TJ began. "You and I have made a lot of progress since we left farming and started this operation."

Al smiled, "Well TJ, we've pulled together with the combined strengths of your administrative skills and my marketing savvy."

"Now that you mention my administrative skills, Al, I'd like to focus some of those skills on marketing. We've had great feedback from our customers, thanks to an excellent product and your involvement. I'd like to know how much each of our customers contributes to the ice cream division's profits as well as how much it is costing us to do business with each. Do you have any way of finding that information?"

"I've kept a diary of sales orders and lunch expenses. Is that what you mean?"

"Well, that's a start, Al. I would like to know what it costs us to keep a customer versus the revenues we make off that customer. What other costs are incurred to make a sale and deliver the product to our customers?"

Al thought for a moment, "Well there are the usual shipping costs that Bakerview normally pays. I suppose we should also include the cost of Jenna's time to take the orders."

"How about the 'Scoop to Win' ice cream promotional events you've put on for our larger clients?"

"Oh yeah.....you know what, I'll bet Pat has all of this cost information right at her fingertips. I'll go talk to her right away."

"Great idea, Al. Do you suppose you and Pat could have something for next Monday's weekly meeting?"

"Certainly!"

Pat works overtime on many days to ensure that management is provided with timely, accurate and relevant information. She knows that the information TJ and Al have requested is relevant to determining profitability. First she made a list of the top customers that provided 80% of the company's sales volume and then downloaded data from the computer that provided information on product line sales and cost of sales for each of the customers. (See Customer Analysis, Table 4, Appendix). As a next step to determine customer profitability, she identified all activities that took place in order to make the sales to customers. Then she identified what it costs to perform each of these activities for all customers and the total amount of activities for the year. (See Table 1.)

Table 1

ACTIVITY ANALYSIS			
	Total Cost	Cost Driver	Annual Activity
Sales calls	$ 27,000	Number of calls	225
Taking orders	$ 40,000	Number of orders	450
Delivery costs	$ 32,000	Kilometres driven	15,000
Promotional events	$ 10,000	Number of events	2
Commissions	$142,000	Sales volume (litres)	1,400,000
Warehousing	$ 35,000	Sales volume (litres)	1,400,000
Expedited deliveries	$ 1,200	Expedited delivery	4

Pat then calculated the levels of activity that related to each customer. (See Table 2.)

Table 2

Activity Analysis by Customer							
	AJ's Market	Buy High Foods	Cal's Café	Rina's Discount Foods	Sharon's on Sixth	CJ's Produce	Groceries 'n More
Number of calls	10	70	10	70	12	12	12
Number of orders	12	106	12	110	60	12	48
Kilometres driven	200	6310	270	1640	1080	430	2070
Number of events		1		1			
Sales dollar	$7,813	$2,225,500	$ 3,181	$2,009,450	$335,930	$12,377	$ 77,238
Sales volume (litres)	1,850	531,000	770	478,000	80,400	2,980	18,410
Expedited delivery		3				1	

TOO MUCH INVENTORY!

While inventory is necessary to fulfill production demands for ice cream, Carly Sims, the production supervisor, does not want too much of it. The ingredients for ice cream have a short self life and spoiled inventory results in increased expenses for her department. Plus, overstocked inventory translates into more storage requirements. In April when the production department builds stock to satisfy increased demands for ice cream in the summer, the warehouse could barely hold the supply of ingredients required for production.

Carly is also very particular that there are enough ingredients on hand to maintain production lines. Stock shortages of any ingredient would result in production stops until the ingredients arrived. While she realizes that ingredients required to fill any unplanned shortages could be expedited, express delivery rates are sometimes twice the price of regular delivery. Therefore she and Jim, the purchaser in the division, always make sure that there is an adequate supply of safety stock on hand for those ingredients that are the most difficult to source.

Some ingredients are readily available. Milk, for instance, is purchased directly from Al and TJ's sons who acquired the family dairy farming business from their fathers in 1990. It is shipped to Bakerview's ice cream division on a daily basis and held in storage tanks at the plant. Additional storage is available at the dairy farming operation. Cream, the byproduct of Bakerview's fluid milk processing division, is transported from the milk processing plant in the next building. Jim coordinates the transfer of cream from the fluid milk division to the ice cream division. This, along with the occasional outside purchase of cream due to internal shortages, increases the ordering cost for cream.

"Vanilla is in short supply due to problems with vanilla crops in supplying countries."

Carly is mostly concerned with purchasing vanilla, variegate sauce and particulate. Vanilla is in short supply due to problems with vanilla crops in supplying countries. As a result, it has been a challenge to source reliable supplies of vanilla. Jim at times spends a number of hours sending emails and talking to suppliers on the phone to purchase the vanilla that is required to produce all of Bakerview's ice cream flavours. Variegate sauce and particulate suppliers also require more processing time as the only source of these products is not reliable. The current supplier does not always have enough in stock to supply Bakerview. Therefore Carly has requested that Jim ensure adequate amounts of vanilla, variegate sauce and particulate are always available by making sure an additional week's supply is in stock.

Jim and Carly work with Pat to determine the optimal ordering procedures that would ensure adequate supplies of ingredients without overstocking the inventory. They must also take into consideration the storage requirements and capacities of the plant. The company uses 10,000, 20,000 and 2,000 litre tanks to store cream, fluid milk, and sucrose respectively. The cooler in the warehouse has a capacity to hold barrels containing up to 8000 litres of any combination of vanilla, particulate and variegate sauce. The sauces have a shelf life of up to 40 days if stored in a temperature-controlled environment. The main warehouse could store a maximum of 3000 kilograms of dry milk powder.

For the moment, Carly and Jim are most concerned about peak production periods between April and September. Pat has created the following table of inventory procurement and carrying costs. (See Table 3.)

Table 3

INGREDIENTS INVENTORY COSTS							
INGREDIENT	Quantity	Rate	Per	Ingredient Cost	Number of Purchase Orders (6 months)	Cost per Purchase Order	OrderLead Time (days)	Carrying Cost Per Unit (6 months)
Cream	109,087	$4.00	litre	$436,348	26	$ 90.00	1	$ 1.50
Sucrose	49,105	$0.65	litre	$ 31,918	26	$ 260.00	3	$ 9.00
Stabilizer & emulsifier	2,080	$3.50	litre	$ 7,280	3	$ 220.00	7	$ 12.50
Fluid milk	1,577	$58.20	hectolitre+	$ 91,805	26	$ 4.00	1	$ 1.50
Milk powder	17,006	$5.30	kilogram	$ 90,132	6	$ 105.00	7	$ 5.00
Vanilla	6,169	$70.00	litre	$431,816	5	$ 780.00	10	$ 22.50
Variegate sauce	29,535	$6.00	litre	$177,210	5	$ 450.00	5	$ 22.50
Particulate	8,778	$7.00	litre	$ 61,446	6	$ 250.00	5	$ 22.50

One of the tasks of a management accountant is to analyze and control costs to ensure an acceptable level of profitability. Costs should be controlled to ensure resources are expended where they have the most impact. Two areas of focus in this module are:

- Costs incurred in marketing and providing products to customers
- Maintaining inventory levels.

- A 'customer-centric' organization focuses on the wants and needs of the customer while at the same time maintaining profitability. It is beneficial for an organization to assess the revenues each customer contributes to the income of the company and to control the costs incurred in generating those revenues.

- The optimal level of inventory to have in stock is the amount that allows the organization to satisfy customer demand and at the same time minimizes the costs associated with acquiring and keeping inventory. A management accountant must consider the many factors that affect inventory costs to ensure the demand for inventory is satisfied.

Activity 1

Determine each customer's contribution to Bakerview Dairies ice cream division profits by preparing a customer profitability spreadsheet that calculates revenues and costs for each customer illustrated in this module. Which customers are profitable? Which are not profitable. Should Bakerview discontinue selling to unprofitable customers or should the company find other ways of controlling costs to make these customers profitable?

Activity 2

What does it currently cost Bakerview Dairies' ice cream division to maintain ingredients inventories from April to September? What would it cost to maintain ingredients inventories if an economic order quantity (EOQ) decision model is applied during this period? Prepare a table illustrating current costs, economic order quantity, and projected costs using an EOQ model. Based on the proposed EOQs the table should also include columns for:

- Number of orders per year
- How long it will take to consume the order quantity
- Reorder point

Do the proposed order times take into consideration the shelf life of the ingredients? Will the ice cream division's storage facilities have the capacity to hold the inventories you are proposing under the EOQ model? What are the limitations of using the EOQ decision model for the ice cream division?

To reduce the computational complexity for this activity, use a 180-day period for April to September.

A P P E N D I X :   C U S T O M E R   A N A L Y S I S

Table 4

CUSTOMER ANALYSIS

CUSTOMER	AJ's Market			Buy High Foods			Cal's Café			Rina's Discount Foods			Sharon's on Sixth			CJ's Produce			Groceries 'n More		
SALES	Litres	Unit	Dollars	Litres	Unit	Dollars	Litres	Unit	Dollars	Litres	Unit	Dollars	Litres	Unit	Dollars	Litres	Unit	Dollars	Litres	Unit	Dollars
Vanilla	1,050	$4.05	$4,253	250,000	$3.96	$990,000	520	$4.05	$2,106	245,000	$3.96	$970,200	43,000	$3.96	$170,280	1,750	$4.05	$7,088	9,800	$4.05	$39,690
Moose Madness	560	4.30	2,408	198,500	4.25	843,625	250	4.30	1,075	135,000	4.25	573,750	24,000	4.25	102,000	1,230	4.30	5,289	7,560	4.30	32,508
Chai High	240	4.80	1,152	82,500	4.75	391,875	-	4.80	-	98,000	4.75	465,500	13,400	4.75	63,650	-	4.80	-	1,050	4.80	5,040
TOTAL	1,850		$7,813	531,000		$2,225,500	770		$3,181	478,000		$2,009,450	80,400		$335,930	2,980		$12,377	18,410		$77,238
COST OF SALES																					
Vanilla	1,050	$2.91	$3,056	250,000	$2.91	$727,500	520	$2.91	$1,513	245,000	$2.91	$712,950	43,000	$2.91	$125,130	1,750	$2.91	5,093	9,800	$2.91	$28,518
Moose Madness	560	3.40	1,904	198,500	3.40	674,900	250	3.40	850	135,000	3.40	459,000	24,000	3.40	81,600	1,230	3.40	4,182	7,560	3.40	25,704
Chai High	240	3.28	787	82,500	3.28	270,600	-	3.28	-	98,000	3.28	321,440	13,400	3.28	43,952	-	3.28	-	1,050	3.28	3,444
TOTAL			$5,747			$1,673,000			$2,363			$1,493,390			$250,682			$9,275			$57,666
Gross Margin			$2,066			$552,500			$818			$516,060			$85,248			$3,102			$19,572

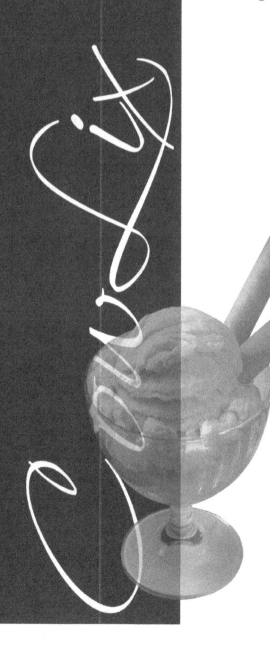

Bakerview Dairies

Module 9
Pricing for Profits

EMPHASIS AND OUTCOMES

The emphasis of this module is on target costing and cost-plus pricing methods.

At the end of this module you should be able to:
- Calculate the target cost of a product.
- Explain situations where use of the cost-plus pricing method is appropriate.

SANTA SWIRL...

"Santa Swirl....that's what we'll call it. We'll make it with green peppermint and red cinnamon sauces combined with a mixture of pecans and walnuts."

Al Haagen, the Marketing Director of the ice cream division of Bakerview Dairies, is discussing the latest ice cream flavour that Barney Larouche, the ice cream Mix Master, has created. Al is in a meeting with TJ Conner (President), Pat Duco (Controller) and Jared Benot (Operations Manager) to present his innovative idea of introducing Santa Swirl to the market.

"Jared's told me that from mid September to late November the plant only operates at around 60% capacity," Al continues. "We have idle resources available for production during that time. We could run this as a trial this year and if it turns out to be a success, we can do it again next year. Jared, how much idle capacity do we have in late September to December to produce Santa Swirl?"

"Remember that we expect to generate about a 10% return on our investment."

"After taking into consideration any possible increase in demand in our other product lines, about 100,000 litres, Al," Jared replied. "Have you thought about what the addition of this product will do to our other lines? We don't want to jeopardize the other flavours by adding this one."

"Well, Jared, according to my focus group sessions and discussions with retailers, there shouldn't be a change in the demand for our existing products. We would market this as a seasonal novelty. Our market research shows that our existing sales will not be affected. In fact, we could increase our revenue by selling around 80,000 litres of Santa Swirl during the months of November and December."

"What about the selling price, Al? What kind of margins will we be generating," asks Pat.

Pat Duco, who is the ice cream division's controller, naturally takes a more pragmatic approach to Al's idea. "Remember that we expect to generate about a 10% return on our investment."

"You're right, Pat and that's why I called this meeting. I think that this can be a profitable strategy, but we need to work through some numbers." Al passes out a costing report to the attendees and continues. "Table 1 lists all of the ingredients costs for 1000 litres of Santa Swirl. This is based on Barney's recipe and the standard costs we use for the other flavours. I priced out the sauces and particulates with our suppliers."

Table 1

STANDARDS FOR MIX AND COST OF MATERIALS (per 1000 litres)				
Frozen measure*	1000	litres	Santa Swirl	
Ingredients	Price	Per	% in mix	Cost per 1000
Cream	$4.00	litre	12.5%	$500.00
Sucrose	$0.65	litre	5.8%	$37.38
Stabilizer & emulsifier	$3.50	litre	0.25%	$8.75
Fluid milk	$58.20	hectolitre+	17.5%	$101.85
Milk powder	$5.30	kilogram	2.0%	$106.00
Vanilla	$70.00	litre	0.5%	$350.00
Variegate sauce	$7.50	litre	9.5%	$712.50
Particulate	$7.00	litre	2.0%	$140.00
Overrun	$0.00		50.0%	$0.00
Cost per 1000 litres			**100.0%**	**$1,956.48**

*1000 litres of ice cream starts with 500 litres of liquid measure. Overrun (the addition of air in the production process) of 100% results in 1000 litres of finished product.

+a hectolitre is equal to 100 litres

"Direct labour costs are $32.41 per hour and we estimate it will take 24 hours to make a 4000-litre batch. The only other direct cost is packaging which will be $0.17 per litre. To generate interest in the product, I thought we could let existing products bear all fixed costs. This strategy will allow us to reduce the introductory price of Santa Swirl to around $3.35, which is lower than the existing specialty ice cream prices. Therefore the only additional costs to consider are listed in Table 2."

Table 2

ADDITIONAL INDIRECT MANUFACTURING COSTS		
	Cost	Per
Plant utilities	$102.00	Batch
Equipment maintenance	$ 97.00	Batch
Quality control inspections	$184.00	Inspection
Inspections per batch	3	
ADDITIONAL OPERATING COSTS		
Design costs	$ 5,500	80,000 litres
Variable marketing costs	$ 0.05	litre
Distribution	$ 2,686	80,000 litres
Introductory marketing campaign	$30,000	

Pat shows some concern over Al's approach, "We don't want to be overly optimistic, Al. While we normally expect a 6% target operating income on sales revenues, we should place a higher expectation for return on this one because we aren't including all fixed costs."

"What type of return should we expect?"

"Taking into account only the additional fixed costs directly related to this product, we should have at least a 10% return on this product's selling price," Pat answers.

TJ has been content to listen to the discussion up to this point. However, as co-owner, he wants to ensure that his investment in the company is providing an adequate return. "What about the return on our investment, Pat. I'd like to see at least a 12% return on our investment. I believe Al has a good idea, but I don't want to price the product low just for the sake of using idle capacity."

"TJ, that means we determine a markup based on product cost, not on consumer demand," Pat replies. "If we take that approach we must choose an appropriate cost base to use and the amount of markup to ensure an adequate return on investment."

"You're the expert, Pat. Could you have that ready by……"

"Tomorrow, right….?"

Pat is aware that management trusts her ability to efficiently provide relevant information. After the meeting she reviews both the manufacturing costs and the general expenses incurred for the company. She develops several product cost bases for Santa Swirl. These are based on incremental costs which are applied directly to the cost of Santa Swirl. She wants to develop markup percentages for each cost, being careful to adjust the markup to provide a minimum 12% return on this investment.

YOU ARE IN CONTROL

An effective product price takes into consideration both the product costs and product demand in the marketplace. Setting a price too high will reduce the product demand while reducing the price beyond product costs threatens company profits. The management accountant forms a team of functional managers in marketing, product development and manufacturing in order to determine an appropriate selling price for the product that attains company targeted profit margins.

Activity 1

Target Costing and Target Pricing: Al feels that Bakerview's ice cream division should be able to sell Santa Swirl for $4.00 per litre. Assess the feasibility of meeting Pat's condition that this product yields a minimum of 10% return on sales and 12% return on the investment in Santa Swirl. Use the cost figures that Al has provided in Tables 1 and 2. Discuss the following:

- Does this price provide the targeted return of 10% of the selling price and provide at least a 12% return on investment?
- In your opinion, should the company increase the price?
- What are your specific recommendations for the division if you want to further increase the profit?

Activity 2

In your opinion do you think this company should be using a cost plus pricing approach? Discuss your reasoning.

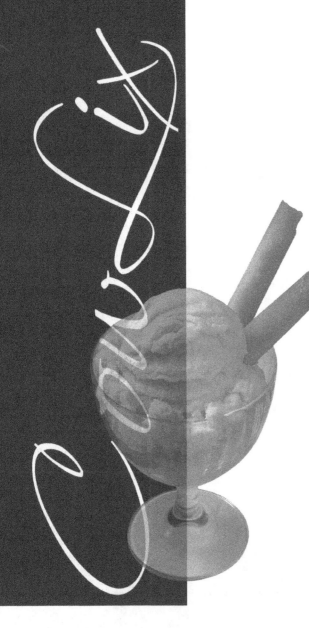

Bakerview Dairies

Module 10
Investing for Profits

EMPHASIS AND OUTCOMES

The emphasis of this module is on capital budgeting using the net present value method.

At the end of this module you should be able to:
- Assess investment projects using the net present value method.
- Explain quantitative and qualitative factors that should be considered when assessing investment projects.
- Discuss the advantages and disadvantages of payback and internal rate of return methods.

MAINTAINING QUALITY

Bakerview Dairies' ice cream division has been producing Cowlix natural brand ice cream for over a decade. The company's three flavours; Vanilla, Moose Madness and Chai High have been marketed to local merchants and major grocery chains throughout Canada. The operations department of the company maintains high standards in processing, resulting in a quality product that is in demand.

To maintain quality standards at low costs the operations department is constantly monitoring its processes. Care is taken to ensure that material handling costs are minimized as batches flow through the production line. Many of the workers are trained in a variety of jobs from blending to packaging, resulting in a plant that is flexible in its operations. Total quality management practices are actively pursued to eliminate defects and reduce plant down time due to machine failure.

The company relies on its equipment to perform the required tasks to produce ice cream that not only satisfies customer tastes but also exceeds health standards. The company that services the ice cream division's equipment has just completed the monthly preventative maintenance review and has informed Jared Benot, the Operations Manager for the division, that the barrel freezers are showing stress cracks. Jared is now notified that if the barrel freezers are not replaced within the next three months, the production line could experience temperature fluctuations resulting in heat shock to the final product.

Ice cream manufacturers are well acquainted with the term 'heat shock.' When producing ice cream, it is important to harden it as quickly as possible. If the mixture is exposed to temperature variations, the mixture freezes into larger ice crystals that create a granular texture instead of the smooth texture that is associated with quality ice cream. Ensuring consistent temperatures throughout the production process is vital.

Barrel freezers are an integral part of producing smooth textured ice cream. After the ingredients for ice cream are blended, pasteurized and homogenized, the mix is cooled to 0° C and pumped into the barrel freezers which freeze and whip air into the frozen mixture in about 30 seconds. Rotating blades within the barrel freezer constantly rotate to scrape the ice from the freezer surface. At the same time dashers help to break down the ice and add air to the ice cream. The addition of air, called 'overrun' is a normal process in the ice cream industry, where as much as 50% of the completed product can contain air. Air is necessary to keep the ice cream from freezing into a solid block of ice.

"Jared is keen to find a replacement for the barrel freezers, as a malfunction can ruin a batch of ice cream and shut down production lines."

Jared is keen to find a replacement for the barrel freezers, as a malfunction can ruin a batch of ice cream and shut down production lines. The current equipment was purchased ten years ago at a cost of $120,000. It was amortized over a 12-year period using the straight-line method, assuming no expected salvage value. Jared believes that this equipment could be sold for $13,000 to an equipment recycling facility. He contacted the company's equipment supplier who has provided Jared with two replacement alternatives.

Alternative 1

The first alternative is model BQW SDN 18/15. The supplier has provided the following information to Jared. (See Table 1.)

Table 1

Alternative 1 – BQW SDN 18/15 – Barrel freezer	
BQW SDN 18/15 – Barrel freezer - Price	$130,000
Estimated life	10 years
Installation cost	$12,500
On-site training	$1,300
Estimated salvage value	$10,000

The sales agent has convinced Jared that model BQW SDN 18/15 is designed for more convenient cleaning which could reduce annual setup and maintenance costs by $17,000 and $10,000 respectively. However, Jared is quite certain that this alternative will utilize 5% more electrical power to operate the plant. This would mean that the utilities expenses will increase by $7,000 annually.

Alternative 2

The second alternative is to purchase the BQW Model V barrel freezer. See Table 2 for data on price, estimated life, installation cost, on-site training cost, maintenance costs and estimated salvage value. BQW Model V uses older technology to freeze the ice cream which will result in $20,000 of major repairs in year five. The freezer is expected to last for 13 years.

Table 2

Alternative 2 – BQW Model V – Barrel freezer	
BQW Model V – Barrel freezer - Price	$90,000
Estimated life	13 years
Installation cost	$8,500
On-site training	$1,300
Estimated salvage value	$5,000
Maintenance costs at end of fifth year	$20,000

Jared is convinced that the BQW Model V does not use as much electricity as the present freezer. Therefore it is estimated that the cost of annual utilities will decrease by $7000. Maintenance will also be reduced by $10,000 annually. The setup costs will remain the same as the present level.

WHICH METHOD TO USE?

Jared takes the information to Pat in accounting. According to his calculations, the BQW SDN 18/15 is the better investment. With an investment of $130,000 and annual savings of $20,000[1], the payback is 6.5 years. The BQW Model V requires an overall investment of $110,000 with an annual savings of $14,000[2]. The payback, according to Jared is close to 8 years. Once he receives the confirmation from Pat, he is going to fill out the purchase order for the BQW SDN 18/15.

"You may be making the right decision, Jared, but I think we should look at all of the facts before a final decision is made."

"What else is there to consider, Pat? We want to recoup as quickly as possible the investment in the assets we purchase, right?"

"That's right, but we want to consider all of the costs in light of the expected return on our investments. We want at least an 8% return on our capital investments. We should also consider the tax implications of the purchase. The capital cost allowance of 30% on this type of investment will reduce income and taxes. Our marginal tax rate is 40%....."

Jared knows this meeting is going to last longer than he had planned.

YOU ARE IN CONTROL

A considerable portion of a firm's investment is in fixed assets. These assets are required to produce profits for the organization. Decisions made to purchase fixed assets or to invest in long term projects will affect the company for a number of years in the future. Therefore, it is important that all factors relating to the investment are considered before an investment decision is made. A credible capital budgeting methodology is used to assess these factors.

Activity 1 Determine the net present value of both freezers. Based on the net present value method, which freezer should be purchased?

---

[1] $17,000(Setup) + $10,000 (maintenance) - $7,000(utilities)

[2] $4,000(utilities) + $10,000 (maintenance)

Activity 2   The payback and internal rate of return methods are often used to assess capital investments. Would either of these methods be suitable tools for assessing the purchase of a barrel freezer for the ice cream division? Why or why not?

Activity 3   Which capital budgeting methodology provides a more accurate assessment of the investment? What qualitative factors should be considered before making the final decision?

Bakerview Dairies

Module 11
Evaluating Success

EMPHASIS AND OUTCOMES

This module focuses on the assessment of the performance of an entity as well as its units by employing the management tools, such as benchmarking, the balanced scorecard and responsibility accounting. The module also focuses on the use of the quantitative measures, return on investment, residual income and return on sales as well as appropriate qualitative factors.

At the end of this module you should be able to:
- Develop measures for evaluating the performance of an organization.
- Assess an organization's performance using financial and non-financial data.
- Perform benchmarking using Industry Canada's Performance Plus website.
- Explain the Balanced Scorecard methodology of translating an organization's strategy into measurable objectives and initiating action plans to meet the objectives.
- Apply an integrated approach to problem solving by incorporating the findings and recommendations in Modules 1 through 10, and plan for the future.

HOW DID WE DO?

Every year, in March, before Bakerview Dairies' ice cream division's production gears up for the busy summer months, the management team goes to the local ski resort. While their families spend most of the three-day retreat taking advantage of the local spring skiing conditions, the managers meet to review the past year's performance and plan for the future.

"Pat also wants to quantify the organization's success with an analysis of the division's profitability."

Al Haagen and TJ Conner have invested in a time share complex at the resort that provides many of the amenities required for a management retreat. The management staff and their families are treated to a weekend away while Al and TJ consider the opportunity as an investment for the future of their company. They are able to spend much time with the management team reviewing the results of the operations of the previous year and planning for the next year.

TJ feels that it has been a fairly good year for the division. He wants to reward the managers fairly for the work they have contributed to producing and marketing Bakerview's high quality, natural ice cream. He has asked Pat Duco to present the annual report to the management team. Along with the annual summary of income (see Table 1), Pat also wants to quantify the organization's success with an analysis of the division's profitability.

Table 1

BAKERVIEW DAIRIES - COWLIX ICE CREAM DIVISION FOR YEAR ENDED DECEMBER 31	
Litre Sales	1,400,000
Sales	$ 5,873,000
Manufacturing Costs	
Direct Manufacturing Costs	$ 3,013,880
Manufacturing Overhead	$ 1,658,800
Total Manufacturing Costs	4,672,680
Gross Margin	$ 1,200,320
Selling and Administrative Expenses	$ 794,060
Operating Income	$ 406,260

Evaluating the success of Bakerview Dairies' ice cream division for the past year is an important topic of this meeting. Pat has researched several different methods for evaluating overall performance for the division and decided to use the following three measures:

- Return on investment (ROI)
- Residual income (RI)
- Return on sales (ROS)

Each of these measures provides a slightly different approach to profitability analysis. Pat wants to provide an accurate assessment of how well the division has utilized its investment of $2,500,000 in assets. The division expects a return of 8% on its investments.

HOW DO WE BENCHMARK?

During her preparation of the annual report, Pat is also considering the possibility of creating benchmark figures for presentation to the management team. The concept of benchmarking has been discussed a number of times in the past year. The management team wants to benchmark, but does not know where to start. The dairy products industry is limited regionally, with local competition closely guarding its profit margins and processes.

"Pat is also considering the possibility of creating benchmark figures for presentation to the management team."

Last month, the local chapter of Pat's professional accounting body provided a one-day seminar on benchmarking. Pat was eager to learn more about this valuable tool and attended the event. One of the tools she was shown in the seminar was Industry Canada's Performance Plus website from which she learned the steps to research the dairy products industry in general and more specifically to find financial details on the ice cream and novelties industry in Canada. She is eager to share her knowledge with the managers by presenting them with useful benchmarking data.

WE NEED MORE THAN JUST NUMBERS...

In her final preparation for the meeting, Pat also wants to spend fifteen minutes presenting the advantages of implementing the balanced scorecard approach to assessing the division's strategy. She knows that presenting financial data is not enough to assess the division's success and feels that the balanced scorecard tool will provide a better focus by translating the mission and strategy of the firm into measurable objectives for planning, evaluation and communication.

Her plan is to present the benefits of the balanced scorecard and persuade management to implement this tool in the coming year.

YOU ARE IN CONTROL

The management accountant is responsible for implementing accurate costing systems and for compiling and reporting the data that is gathered using these systems. This information can be useful in evaluating the performance of a company and its management team. Providing this service is an ongoing challenge for the management accountant who must find performance measures that accurately report to the organization's stakeholders both quantitative and qualitative factors.

Activity 1

Prepare ROI, RI and ROS calculations for Bakerview Dairies' ice cream division. What does each measure suggest about the division's profitability? Which of these measures should Pat present in the annual report? Do you agree with TJ that the division has had a profitable year? Explain your answer.

Activity 2

Industry Canada Performance Plus Analysis

Industry Canada's Performance Plus website at http://sme.ic.gc.ca/epic/internet/inpp-pp.nsf/en/Home is an interactive on-line financial performance tool that can be used by firms to benchmark their performance with the industry. It allows the user to enter a company's financial data and compare it to industry averages.

Browse the site to learn more about Performance Plus. The 'What is Performance Plus?' and 'How to Use Performance Plus' options provide an overview of this site. The 'View a Sample Case' option gives a detailed explanation of how organizations can build a profile of their company. When you have learned more about this tool, perform a quick analysis of the ice cream industry by taking the following steps:

- Select the 'Build Your Own Profile' option.

- Select the most recent North American Industry Classification System (NAICS) option available.[1]
- When you arrive at the 'Build Your Own Profile' screen, enter the following data:
  - REPORT CRITERIA
    - Would you like to create a customized report? – Select 'No'
    - Geographic Area – Select your province (you should also do a profile of Canada)
    - Business Type – All Businesses
    - Expense Data Units - % of Total Revenue
    - When you have entered all the data for this screen, click 'Continue'
  - INDUSTRY SELECTION
    - Enter the NAICS Number: 31152 - 'Ice Cream and Frozen Dessert Manufacturing' (Note the extensive list of different industries that are represented in the NAICS listing)
    - Click 'Create Report'
  - REPORT SETUP
    - Accept the criteria as listed
    - Click 'Create Report'

- When you have created the report, select and save the data to an Excel spreadsheet.

Questions you should be able to answer:

- What is the significance of this data to Bakerview Dairies?
- In which revenue range does Bakerview Dairies fall?
- Note the NAICS category: 'Ice Cream and Frozen Dessert Manufacturing.' How relevant is the data to Bakerview Dairies' ice cream division? How would some of these figures change if this category only reported data for ice cream manufacturers? (Do you think that direct labour and purchases percentages would be higher or lower?)
- Identify the data that will be useful for evaluating the ice cream division's performance.

Activity 3

Pat wants to prepare a fifteen-minute PowerPoint presentation to the management team on how to use the balanced scorecard approach to address the key objectives, initiate appropriate action plans and assess strategy. The purpose of her presentation is to emphasize the merits of the approach and to acquire management's commitment to develop the balanced scorecard. She would like to provide the team with some useful

---

[1]North American Industry Classification System (NAICS) - Statistics Canada's standardized coding system for grouping businesses engaged in similar types of activity into non-overlapping industry categories. At time of writing, 2002 codes were the latest statistics available.

examples as well. She wants you to provide the following information for her presentation:

- What is the balanced scorecard?
- How can it benefit the ice cream division?
- A listing of each of the four perspectives. For each perspective provide:
    - Two objectives
    - A quantifiable measure for each of the planned objectives
    - A target for each objective
    - An initiative that the company will undertake to meet each objective

Develop the objectives, measures and action plans that are specific to your understanding of Bakerview Dairies' ice cream division. To help you with your presentation, visit the Balanced Scorecard Institute's website at the following address to find current information on the balanced scorecard:

- www.balancedscorecard.org/basics/bsc1.html

The Balanced Scorecard –Financial Perspective				
#	Objective	Measure	Target	Initiative
1				
2				

The Balanced Scorecard –Customer Perspective				
#	Objective	Measure	Target	Initiative
1				
2				

The Balanced Scorecard –Internal Business Process Perspective				
#	Objective	Measure	Target	Initiative
1				
2				

The Balanced Scorecard –Learning and Growth Perspective				
#	Objective	Measure	Target	Initiative
1				
2				

Activity 4

Prepare a report to Pat Duco, TJ Conner and Al Haagen. Your report should discuss the following:

- What are Bakerview Dairies' ice cream division's key strategic thrusts?
- Has the company been able to successfully implement its strategies?
- What recommendations would you provide the company:
  - For the next quarter?
  - For the next year?
- Provide an action plan outlining the steps the company should take and who should be involved.

Address the issues that have been identified and discussed in the previous modules in your analysis.